"Karsen's knowledge about the online economy is absolutely unmatched. We all have something to learn from his practical examples about how to profit from the new opportunities on the Internet. Karsen also helped me in the online promotion for my income-generating venture Chinofy. I recommend this book both for beginners and for pros wanting to upgrade their skill set."
**— Bo-Erik Abrahamsson, Oxford University Scholar and Founder of Chinofy. Formerly Strategy Associate at Twitter**

"Brilliant and thorough. From making money online to outsourcing your business and life, it's all here. Whether you're looking for complete financial independence, more free time, or knowledge about online business models, this book will change your life."
**— Alex Scott, Retail Team Lead at Amazon. MBA from London Business School and previously at Deloitte Consulting and General Electric**

"Finally, a more applicable replacement for 50 Cent's *Get Rich or Die Tryin'*. Karsen shows that there is more to the Internet than just funny cat videos with his must-have guide for anyone who wants to leverage this technology to achieve a fulfilling lifestyle. Recommended for everyone pursuing the freedom of having more positive cash flow as an entrepreneur or an employee."
**— Michal Duchacek, Online Marketing Manager at Expedia.com and travel enthusiast. Previously at P&G and McKinsey & Co.**

"This is a book that reveals the new world which the Internet is creating. Karsen has produced a fantastic piece of work to explain the state of the digital revolution to date."
**— Roger Lo, Senior Business Planning and Operations Analyst at Yahoo. Co-Founder of Jumpstart Program**

i

"Having known Karsen for as long as I have, I can say that he has superbly combined 'Life Skills', tech savviness and commercial awareness. The book's value and insights far exceed the small price tag. Your return on investment is guaranteed to skyrocket."

**— Songnian Zhou, Consultant at IBM. Previously at Bain & Co. and Morgan Stanley**

"Karsen is one of the most inspiring and driven people I have ever encountered. He has accomplished more goals at his age than most people do in a lifetime — his book gives you true inspiration to set goals and exceed them!"

**— Magnus Lysell, Corporate Finance at Wingefors Invest venture capital fund. Previously at American Express and H&M**

"What I love about Karsen is his boldness and result-oriented mindset that he brings to any situation. I witnessed him taking immediate action and driving impactful changes. His enthusiasm, drive and determination are infectious. Karsen has impressed me and I'm sure that the material he presents in this book will do the same for you."

**— Vishal Morjaria, Award-Winning Author, Transformational Speaker and Coach**

"Karsen is the ambassador of the digital economy. He opens your eyes and brings new clarity to the muddled world of making money online by creating actionable guidelines. Embracing change and innovation, Karsen draws on extensive experience and his own recipe for simplicity, fun and results."

**— Naval Kumar, Serial Entrepreneur and Digital Marketing Expert at www.navalkumar.com, www.absem.com and www.dme.academy. Awarded The Authority In Aspiring Entrepreneurs Award by *New York Times* Best-Selling Authors Raymond Aaron and Jack Canfield**

# GET PAID TO PLAY™

## LEVERAGING THE INTERNET
## TO CREATE
## YOUR DESIRED LIFESTYLE

This book is for

_____

## KARSEN CHEUNG

**www.KarsenCheung.com**

**www.GetPaidToPlayBook.com**

# Contents

Foreword                                                              1

1   What If Money Did Not Matter                                      5
    *Creating the lifestyle you desire*
    Financial freedom                                                10
    Time freedom                                                     12
    Geographical freedom                                             14
    Life balance                                                     16

2   The Obvious and the Not-So-Obvious                               19
    *Different ways to monetize the Internet*
    Finding the hottest trends in the new economy                    20
    Online business models                                           22
    Selling physical products online                                 25
    Drop-shipping                                                    27
    E-books and other information products                           29
    Webinars                                                         33
    Online courses                                                   36
    Membership sites                                                 38
    Sales funnel                                                     41
    Google AdSense                                                   46
    Online survey                                                    48
    Financial trading                                                49

3   Buying and Decorating Your Property                              53
    *Building your own website*
    Buying web domain                                                54
    Hosting your domain                                              58

Building your website with WordPress 59
Designing your website 62
Processing payments 65
Creating sales and offer pages 66
Branding 72
Optimizing with web analytics software 75
Optimizing for mobile devices 81

4  Throwing Your Housewarming Party 85
   on a Shoestring
   *Acquiring free traffic to your website*

E-mail marketing and list building 87
Search engine optimization and content marketing 93
Blogging 100
Video marketing 104
Social media marketing 107

5  Throwing Your Housewarming Party in 113
   Style
   *Scaling up with paid advertising*

Paid advertising models 114
Google's suite of advertising products 118
Paid traffic on social media 127
Re-marketing 130
Paid advertising on mobile devices 132

6  Networking With Your Neighbors 135
   *Boosting your income with affiliate marketing*

Leveraging other people's sales funnel 136
Earning commissions through your own site 140
Selecting affiliate vendors and products 142
Establishing joint ventures 146

7   Hiring Housekeepers and Investing          151
    in Robots
        *Outsourcing and automating your business*

    Why you should outsource                    152
    Working *on* business, not *in* business    155
    What you can outsource                       157
    How to find and recruit outsourcers          161
    How to automate your business                163

8   Carpe Diem                                  167
        *Implementing your action plan*

    Visualizing your goals                       169
    Making concrete plans                        170
    Managing your tasks                          175
    Don't overwhelm yourself                     180
    Don't throw all eggs into one basket         183

9   01100001 01100011 01110100                  187
        *Embracing the digital revolution*


Disclaimer                                       193

Glossary                                         195

Acknowledgments                                  198

For more information and FREE bonuses            200

About the Author                                 202

# GET PAID TO PLAY™

# FOREWORD

Raymond Aaron, *New York Times* best-selling author, is one of the most sought-after speakers and teachers in North America and a widely acknowledged real-estate master.

Raymond Aaron is the only author who has ever written both a *Chicken Soup For The Soul*™ book and a *For Dummies*™ book. His best-sellers include *Chicken Soup for the Parent's Soul*, *Chicken Soup for the Canadian Soul*, *Branding Small Business For Dummies* and *Double Your Income Doing What You Love*. He has shared his wisdom on radio and TV for over 20 years, and his achievements have propelled him to the prestigious lists of the Canadian Who's Who and the International Who's Who of Entrepreneurs.

He completed one of the world's toughest races, Polar Race (a 350-mile foot race to the North Magnetic Pole), which inspired his other book, *How You Can Get Rich Without Getting Cold*. He is a member of Mensa, the high-IQ society, and holds an Honors degree from the University of Toronto in Mathematics and Physics.

Freedom is "the state of not being imprisoned or enslaved", and it is one of the most fundamental human endeavors regardless of who you are, where you are from and what your social status is. Many people strive for it all their lives, and yet only a small percentage actually get to experience genuine freedom. Most people still have to do certain things not by choice but out of necessity and the harsh reality of life.

The great news is that technological innovations can now give you opportunities to shape your destiny. In this fascinating book, Karsen draws upon his expertise in the digital economy and Internet marketing to illustrate a future of innovative ways to make money online and to design your ideal lifestyle. His remarkable ability to present the oft-taught subject of online money generation in a refreshing and insightful way is what makes this book so special.

Karsen's book, *Get Paid to Play*™, will take you on an educational and empowering journey. It will provide you with a concise summary of the hottest, profitable trends and a detailed analysis of the return-on-investment of each online business model. The much sought-after guide will help you navigate the gigantic world of the Internet and show you places you have never imagined to be possible.

However, far from a typical get-rich-quick book, the ultimate purpose of *Get Paid to Play*™ is to inspire and impress the concept of life balance upon you. Karsen's book comes from his heart and covers much more than just business principles and marketing techniques. He will challenge you to reassess your life in light of the digital revolution, and to reflect on how you could leverage it to create the lifestyle you desire for yourself and your family.

Full of positive values and encouraging life principles, Karsen's book is a powerful portrayal of what the future holds for people who dare to dream and a compelling call to take action now. With his invaluable advice on life planning and task management, you will be sure to achieve more with less stress.

Regardless of where you are at in your life journey, the pursuit of freedom is what connects us all as humanity. If you wish to transform your life and create your lifestyle of genuine freedom, *Get Paid to Play*™ is exactly for you. I cannot recommend this book highly enough.

*Raymond Aaron*

**GET PAID TO PLAY™**

# 1 - WHAT IF MONEY DID NOT MATTER

## Creating the lifestyle you desire

Too many people in modern-day society still have the mindset of the industrial age, where time has to be traded for money. People who have a lot of money don't usually have much spare time, and vice versa. It is very rare to find those who have both spare time and money. This is rather bizarre: the digital revolution and the information age we are in right now have created endless opportunities for us to move away from the model of trading time for money, yet most people are not aware of how the Internet can be leveraged to generate income and create a comfortable lifestyle. By outlining the different ways to make money via the Internet in this book, my hope is that you can reclaim your time and generate more income, so you can enjoy both time and financial freedom.

The concepts of time and financial freedom might be foreign to you. Time freedom does not mean you don't do anything. It just means you have the freedom to choose what you do and when you do it, because you are not restricted by time commitments such as having a full-time job with fixed hours. Combine this with financial freedom — when you have enough money coming from a passive source of income to cover your expenses and no longer have to trade your time for money — you will have a lot more free time to pursue your passion and interests, and to spend your time, energy and resources on the people and things that really matter to you.

Of course, not everyone's goal is the same. Not everyone is interested in becoming the super wealthy, but I am sure most people would love to have a stable, passive source of income that will, at the same time, allow them to spend more time with their loved ones and enjoy doing the things that they are passionate about. Perhaps for you, this is to travel around the world, to read more books, to play more sports, or to invest quality time in relationships. I am sure that, if money is not a concern, many people would love to spend more time pursuing their passions, chasing their dreams, following their lifelong mission of helping others and making an individual impact on society, all of which will lead to greater personal development and a deeper sense of fulfillment.

Sadly, society has molded people into nine-to-five jobs and certain patterns in life. Walking down these beaten paths and fulfilling other people's expectations on us have limited our imagination. Too many of us are working long hours in jobs that we don't necessarily like and that don't necessarily pay enough, leaving little time, energy and resources to pursue the things that we are passionate about and to create a lifestyle we desire.

This book is exactly for these kinds of people. It is not exclusive to people who want to become millionaires and billionaires, and people who just want to have all the time in the world doing nothing. It is not a get-rich-quick book; rather, it is a book about lifestyle in the digital age — about liberating yourself from the lifestyle predefined by society, and using the Internet as a tool to help you do so.

Building your own lifestyle business is not a get-rich-quick scheme, so you should find reasons that will motivate you. Your motivation and your end goal should not be money. Money is only one of the ways through which you can create a lifestyle you desire. Having all the money in the world will not necessarily make you happy. Think about what makes you truly happy. Think about the kind of life you want. *Then*, think about how money can help you get there and how you can get that money.

In fact, find reasons that are bigger than yourself, such as providing for your family or changing your community or the world. You will then experience and be reminded of a greater sense of purpose whenever you hit an obstacle during your journey as a lifestyle entrepreneur. As you go on this journey, I want you to keep this in mind and know exactly what your motivation is, because having the right mindset will keep you on track and having the right motivation can fuel you a long way.

I have worked on some of the world's most cutting-edge digital marketing campaigns at Expedia, Inc. | Hotels.com. As the top 5 advertising spender on Google, their multimillion-dollar Internet marketing campaigns across all media platforms are taken to a whole new level in terms of investment, optimization and sophistication. Can you imagine what results you and other small and medium businesses can get if you just learn a few key strategies here and implement them into your online business? In addition, from my wide range of experiences with prestigious strategy consulting practices, billion-dollar corporations, venture capital investment funds and fast-growing start-ups (read more in detail at the end of the book), I learned how world-class businesses approach strategy, marketing and the digital revolution. Again, by applying some of these high-end lessons, your own online business will be able to rise above your competitions.

I am currently rapidly building several online businesses for myself and for others, scaling some highly successful campaigns and websites, and trading other people's and my own funds in the financial markets online. And I have been able to do many of the things I love, particularly travelling, with the extra income and cash flow from these online ventures. I am telling you all these not to impress you, but to impress upon you why I am passionate to share my thoughts on this topic with you. My goal is to open your mind to the endless possibilities that the Internet can offer, the new business models in this digital age and how you can make the most of the Internet to gain time and financial freedom. I sincerely want to help and want you to see results too.

In the chapters that follow, I will outline the different ways through which you can make money via the Internet, so you can decide for yourself what is best for you and what will help you achieve your goals. But ultimately, I want to inspire you to move towards a new way of living and to create a lifestyle that allows you to enjoy time and financial freedom. So you no longer have to worry about finding the money to pay your bills. So you don't have to please other people and fulfill others' expectations on you anymore. So you can stop doing the things you don't like and start doing the things you genuinely love. So you can spend more time with your family and friends. So you can pursue your passion and hobbies. So you can live a life you won't regret. Life is too short for you to live out someone else's life. So, join me and explore for yourself how you can leverage the Internet to create the lifestyle you desire.

### Financial freedom

To put it simply, having financial freedom is when your passive income — that is, money you don't have to work actively for — exceeds your expenditure. It means you would still have enough money to sustain your lifestyle even if you don't actively work to generate income. It means not trading your time for money.

Passive income usually comes as the reward of your hard work in the past. For example, once you have put in the work to write a book, the royalties you gain from future book sales, both online and offline, will become your passive income. Alternatively, you can create a best-selling product that will continuously reward you financially. Investing wisely in dividend-paying stocks is another way to create a passive income stream. That's it. Financial freedom can be that simple.

You do not need to be a millionaire to have financial freedom. In fact, if you win $1 million from the lottery now, you will have financial freedom while money is still around. But if you don't generate income on a consistent basis and you only have that $1 million, the money will run out eventually, and you will no longer enjoy that financial freedom. The statistic is that most lottery winners are back to square one financially after 4 years of winning, because they are not generating a consistent income and actually spending more than they make.

Passive income is only one way to build wealth. Your overall wealth also includes your investment portfolio, savings and active income. So, if you want to take it to the next level, you will need to consider investing in a smart way so your wealth can growth. You will also want to have an active income, where you get paid for your work — for example, by giving speeches or delivering workshops, being a consultant to businesses, or having a job. A lot of people choose to have active income on top of their passive income because they feel like they can make more of an impact in a bigger organization, because they enjoy the sophisticated work they do in big corporations, or because they love working in a team and being inspired by others in the organization. The difference is that, if you have a source of passive income, then what you do is not limited by what gives you the active income. You can still choose to walk away from your active income and take a long vacation while not worrying about your finances.

In essence, having financial freedom means that you do not have to work actively on a consistent basis to create income. Your passive income is enough to cover all your expenses, and you have the freedom to pick and choose what you really want to do instead of doing whatever job comes your way to pay the bills. Effectively, you are getting paid to play.

## Time freedom

As opposed to money, there is no way to create more time or to save it up for later. Therefore, as a lifestyle entrepreneur, you need to be selective about what you do with your 24 hours a day. Time freedom, of course, is not about doing nothing at all. In my opinion, time freedom for most people would mean doing the things that really matter to them. Doing things that you truly love and enjoy, rather than being trapped in a job that requires 40 hours or more per week. Choosing what you will do with your time and how you will schedule your day. You might think, "This sounds great, but it's probably only for people who have their own businesses or who are rich." This is not true. Yes, it helps that if you have your own business, you have more control over your working hours. But, more importantly, by optimizing and maximizing your productivity, you can free up your time and spend it on other activities, whether it's working for more active income, building a source of passive income, writing a book, or going to tango classes.

To optimize your productivity, the first and foremost is to be selective about how you spend your time. Time is our most valuable commodity, and there is simply no way to recover the time lost to idleness, to fulfilling other's expectations and to doing things we regret. Learn to say "no", and always prioritize your goals and tasks. Second, having an effective task management system will give you a clear idea of what you need to do next, giving you peace of mind because you don't have to spend your downtime thinking repeatedly about what else there is to do. It also helps you to map your progress and puts each task into perspective, so you don't lose focus of the big picture. I will cover these concepts in more detail in Chapter 8.

A principle that is highly relevant to this topic is the "80/20 principle". Vilfredo Pareto, an Italian economist who has done extensive research into how most things in life, society and nature work, proposed that 80% of the results come from 20% of input. There is always 20% of work that can generate 80% of the desired results.

Say, you are learning to play the drum set. In order to perform a song with your band, you need to learn the basic drumming skills, the tempo of the song and the basic beat variations. These are essentially your 20%. Everything else — the fills, the fancy throws of drumsticks or elaborate stage performance — are all nice-to-haves but not strictly necessary. These extras are not considered part of the 20%, because you can still play the basic beats that keep up at the right tempo as the band performs. Of course, you will need to practice and perfect your skills, but you have essentially achieved 80% of the results. The embellishments are what you learn after you have mastered the first 20%. There is no point in practicing the different ways to throw your drumsticks before you can play the beats. Identify the 20% of work that will have the most immediate or the greatest impact, so you can achieve maximum output in the least amount of time.

## Geographical freedom

By this point, you probably can't wait to achieve financial and time freedom. What if I now introduce you to the concept of geographical freedom? Imagine working from your laptop on a beach, somewhere up in the mountains, at home, on a road trip, or in a nice resort — does this sound too good to be true? Not if you build your business and make money online because, as long as there is Internet connection, you can do your work whenever and wherever you like. Most importantly, if you automate your business, your income-generating process will become a lot more passive. You could take long holidays, climb the Himalayas or go skydiving, and not have to worry about making money actively. Having an automated online business gives you this freedom, because your income will continue to roll in while you are asleep and dreaming about all the possibilities. All you have to do is, every now and then, go online, check how your site is doing, how your marketing campaigns are running, and how many sales you have made, then do the necessary corrections whenever you have time.

Geographical freedom is one of the defining characteristics of the dot com lifestyle. Throughout history, people have always been tied to a geographical location — people who owned castles in medieval times, those who owned massive mansions several hundred years ago, or those who own factories or offices in modern times. Those are the only place where they can do their businesses other than business trips. If they leave the place for too long, they might start missing out on a lot of business opportunities. Moreover, their wealth is not as easily transferable as now. They could not physically take their castles or mansions with them as they traveled, or indeed factories and offices.

Many traditional professions are tied to certain regional qualifications or jurisdictions, and it is not easy to travel around for extended periods of time or move to new places to live. Salaried employees are tied to a certain office where their colleagues are. The digital revolution and the technologies it brings now free us from being tied to one geographical location. As long as you have a laptop and Internet connection, you can travel around and work whenever and wherever you like, unrestricted by time zones and geographical boundaries. As technology continues to develop, the ability to stay connected will transform the way we work and live. It will allow us to be more efficient, more productive and more creative, and the possibilities are truly limitless.

## Life balance

"Work–life balance" is a catch phrase that society uses to juxtapose these two areas of our lives, but this phrase implies that you cannot have a life when you are working, and vice versa. It also reflects the cruel reality that many people are not passionate about their jobs or even dread going to work, to say the least. Instead of work–life balance, why can't it simply be life balance? Life is so much more than just "work" and "non-work". A fulfilling life encompasses many different aspects — professional, social, physical, emotional, spiritual, and so on. And all these aspects need to be in healthy equilibrium. Life is too short to waste at least 9 hours a day (which adds up to 45 hours a week, 2,000 hours a year and 80,000 hours over a 40-year career) doing the things you dread. Just imagine how wonderful it would be to stop doing these things because money is no longer an issue, and how rewarding it is to fill up the newfound time with choice — the choice to pursue your dreams, invest in great relationships and have fun. This is why I am a firm believer of lifestyle entrepreneurship, where all areas of your life are in great harmony.

Yes, you may say that this is too optimistic and idealistic, and I don't blame you for saying so. It is not the first, nor will it be the last, time I hear people complaining about their lives, far too frequently and for far too long. Yet, they don't seem to do anything about it until they look back one day and regret. With the advance of technology and the Internet, it is actually difficult to find a decent excuse as to why you cannot do something about your life. With a little guidance (and hopefully you can find that in this book), you could at least make an attempt. You simply have to broaden your horizon and model the people that are living the life you want to have for yourself. Let me ask you this: How much is life balance worth to you? And how do you even put a price tag on financial, time and geographical freedom for the rest of your life? To me, these things are priceless and worth pursuing. If your answer is similar, then what are you waiting for? Join in on the movement of lifestyle entrepreneurship and get started now!

**GET PAID TO PLAY™**

## 2 - THE OBVIOUS AND THE NOT-SO-OBVIOUS

### Different ways to monetize the Internet

In this information age, knowledge is highly valued. The digital revolution has completely changed the way we work. Digital products and technologies have created new industries and changed how existing industries operate. Look at travel booking: instead of going to your local travel agent in person or giving them a phone call, many websites will now allow you to book flights, hotels and holiday packages, and even compare prices between providers. Instead of buying a thick travel guide from a bookstore, forums such as TripAdvisor allow everyone to participate and access up-to-date information in real time.

In this new economy, we no longer have to trade our time for money. We no longer have to put in a set number of hours for a set amount of money, which gives us the opportunity to pursue financial and time freedom. Try to develop multiple streams of passive income: your initial hard work will be rewarded and you will get paid out over and over again. It is key to have a completely new way of thinking about how you work and how to meet your needs. Essentially, it goes back to how you can earn money in the most effective and efficient way. Again, it is about finding that 20% of work that will give 80% of the desired results — the things that, when done, will have an immediate impact or give the greatest financial results.

## Finding the hottest trends in the new economy

With the constant innovation of technologies and creation of new business models, it is especially important to find what works for you before you can focus on that 20%. Scan the horizon and learn what the newest and hottest trends are in this fast-moving digital age. When a new trend comes up, there tends to be a wave of early adopters and pioneers who are willing to try. Once the trend becomes hot, everyone else will start jumping onto it, making it very competitive. Eventually, the trend will be phased out when new technologies are innovated and new products are created; it will slowly die out and be replaced by newer trends. Therefore, your goal is to identify the hottest trends that will work for you, riding on the trend while it is still hot because, once it is over, you might have to learn something completely new again.

An example is Google AdWords on paid search, which is when advertisers bid for certain search queries to have their ads displayed in a favorable position on Google's search results page when those keywords are searched for. Paid advertising on search engines used to be a very cheap marketing channel to attract visitors from the search results to a certain website. At the time, not everyone had been jumping onto the trend because offline marketing, such as billboard advertising and TV ads, was very dominant. However, pioneering companies such as Amazon and eBay started doing search engine marketing during the early stages of Google AdWords when it was extremely cheap. They invested money to develop technologies around search engine marketing and had become very sophisticated online advertisers. They were able to direct a lot of traffic from Google Search to their websites at relatively low unit cost (cost per click), and that has enabled their businesses to grow to the size they are now. However, if you try to get on to Google AdWords now, 10 years after these early adopters, the unit cost has gone up dramatically, and the market has become highly saturated and competitive. It is very difficult for companies and small businesses who are just starting now to capture those leads at a low cost.

A key principle is to be open-minded, adaptable and willing to try. While it is essential to have a laser focus on what you do and work hard to achieve the best results, it is also vital to keep up with the latest, hottest trends and look out for new opportunities. Look at what other people have achieved and, if you think it could work for you as well, try it out by putting in a small investment. If it starts delivering small but nonetheless significant results, then increase the level of commitment you put into it. Yes, you need to have a clear vision of what you want to achieve, but don't be so stubbornly focused on one thing that you miss out on the big trends that could potentially make or break your business. While Jeff Bezos, CEO of Amazon, was determined about getting the logistics right and creating the biggest e-commerce company in the world, he also made the decision to be an early adopter of Google AdWords. If he hadn't been willing to be open to this opportunity, Amazon would not be the size that it is now.

## Online business models

The Internet has completely revolutionized our lives and is still continuing to do so. But what do you use the Internet for? Most people don't realize that there is much more going on behind what they experience when they surf the Internet, and how they can also take advantage of this great technology to generate income themselves. There are so many ways to make money online that it is impossible to cover them all in detail in just one book. Entering the term "how to make money online" on Google gives more than 500 million results! So, how do you decide what will work best for you?

With such a huge amount of noise out there on this topic, I want to give you a clear overview of the various ways to make money on the Internet in the comfort of your own home. I will present some of the hottest trends and online business models, and show you the effort it takes to be part of those trends and the potential return on investment. Not every business model will give the same amount of return, and the amount of work required from you varies as well. Start by trying out a few different ways and remember that you do not ever have to be locked into one method. Then, adjust your level of commitment depending on the return on investment, and optimize to get the best possible results.

Decide for yourself what works for you and what suits your situation and interests most. There are many ways in which you can make money online, and there is no one magic formula to success. To dip your hands into every single one of these buckets would be too overwhelming, and I do not encourage you to do that at all. While it is important to have a understanding of the different online business models, the best way forward is to focus on a few that you feel most connected with and have the most passion about. If you enjoy writing, perhaps blogging would be a natural starting point. Writing several paragraphs once a week or once every few days is doable, and a lot of people have started and maintained successful and profitable blogs.

To a lot of people, making money online seems such an elusive concept, so distant that they don't think they can also be a part of it, or so technical that they think they need to be a computer programmer. It is important to recognize that the Internet is ultimately a vehicle that will help you to reach your desired destination. Many offline business models can be adapted to work in the online world. For example, if you refer a client to a friend of yours or to a company, you will often get a commission or a referral bonus, because you are giving them a prospective lead and potential sales. Often, they will reach out to you and offer a 10–20% commission for every successful referral. In the online world, the same model operates. This is what we call affiliate marketing. If you are able to drive people to a particular website where they end up making a purchase, then you are bringing new customers to an online business. This is usually accompanied by a commission payout and is an easy way to make money if you do it consistently. Digital products — for example, e-books and online courses — can be reproduced easily and do not need to be delivered physically, so business owners are usually happy to pay a much higher commission (usually anything from 30% to 100%) because the cost for them is lower than if they were to own a physical storefront or courier physical products.

Another way would be to simply sell products — both physical and digital — online, either by creating a store on websites like eBay and Amazon, or by building your own website. It is no different to having a storefront on your local high street or in a shopping mall. What's better is that your online store will be open 24/7, and there is no need to hire staff to manage in-store operations. Rather than having a cashier in store, all you need is a payment button that leads to PayPal to process the transaction.

## Selling physical products online

*Potential result:* Medium

*Input required:* Involves dealing with inventory management, supply chain and product delivery, in addition to marketing and selling products

*Pre-requisite:* Quality suppliers and products

If you already have physical products that you sell offline, an obvious way to boost your income and expand your reach is to sell them online. The Internet has lowered geographical barrier so much that you can buy products from almost anywhere in the world. People's shopping patterns are no longer confined to their local high street or shopping mall in town.

Imagine if you were to expand your retail business across the country. To ensure a good reach, you have to set up storefronts in all the major cities and towns; in some bigger cities, you may need to set up multiple stores in key locations to ensure a good coverage. This equates to a lot of strategic planning, logistical preparations, paying for rent and housekeeping bills, hiring staff and so on to run the stores. Contrast that with an online store, the initial investment of which is very small. For instance, many people that I personally know are building successful 5–6 figure USD businesses simply by listing physical products on eBay and Amazon. Alternatively, you can leverage Google Shopping's Product Listing Ads to generate more laser-targeted traffic to your products. As I will discuss in more detail in Chapter 3, buying and hosting a website domain would probably cost only US$20–80 in total per year, and website design can also be done easily either by yourself at low cost or by a professional for several hundred dollars. After these simple steps, you will already have an online storefront that is accessible to a global audience, not just people in your local area. There is very minimal housekeeping cost, because there is no need to worry about rent, bills and salary for in-store staff as you would for an offline store. Moreover, with an online store, the cost and effort it takes to change your 'store display' are almost negligible. To change the color scheme of your store involves just a few click of buttons — no stripping of wallpaper or painting involved. I don't think I need to convince you of the importance of presentation and displaying your products in an appealing way. The good news is, there is so much more you can experiment with in your online store, and I will cover how to design and optimize your website in more details in the next chapter.

As you have probably experienced yourself, people are doing more and more shopping online. The e-commerce industry is expanding so quickly that it is overtaking a lot of offline shopping, especially as logistic companies are also innovating to deliver products quicker and at a much cheaper rate. Of course, e-commerce will never fully replace offline shopping, but it is proving to become a more important source of income to many retailers. What the Internet has offered is a very affordable way for business owners to sell their physical products online and to increase their profit dramatically, because the cost of selling products online is so much lower than doing so offline. Going back to want I said earlier about finding the hottest trends, e-commerce is definitely a trend that you don't want to be missing out on.

### Drop-shipping

**Potential result:** *Medium*

**Input required:** *Involves sourcing products and promoting them; can be fully systemized, outsourced and automated*

**Pre-requisite:** *Quality suppliers and products*

What if you don't have any physical products to sell? Well, you can become a third-party seller of other supplier's products. This is called drop-shipping, where you contact different suppliers and offer to sell their products as a third party, with the condition that the product is sent straight from the supplier to the customer's shipping address. During this process, you would pay the supplier for the initial costs and be the one processing the payment from the customer. The profit in between will be yours. As opposed to selling your own physical products, there is no need to manage a warehouse, the logistics of shipping or customer refunds. All of these will be dealt with by the supplier, making drop-shipping a scalable way to generate passive income. You will only need to manage a team of outsourcers once you systemize and automate business operations and processes.

The reason that this is a viable business model is because some suppliers are not very tech savvy, and they might not know how to create and monetize their online presence. This is where you can step in and help them to promote their products online. Even if they already have an online store, what you are doing via drop-shipping is increasing their reach and expanding their marketing efforts. This is a win–win situation: the suppliers can increase their sales, and you can make money by marking up the price and taking the profit in between.

You should make sure that your suppliers are happy for you to become their third-party retailer. Not all suppliers will agree to participate in this business model, but you are likely to find some that do, and drop-shipping has proven to be profitable for many lifestyle entrepreneurs.

## E-books and other information products

> ***Potential result:*** *High because of insignificant variable cost or cost of product delivery*
>
> ***Input required:*** *One-off, initial time and financial investment to productize knowledge and information; some maintenance and upgrade later*
>
> ***Pre-requisite:*** *Your own or others' subject matter expertise in profitable niches*

Remember what I said earlier about the information age that we are currently in? Knowledge and content are highly valued in the information age. Therefore, selling information products is one of the best ways to make money online and create passive income. The digital revolution has actually fueled the growth of information product in a substantially beneficial way, particularly in the developing world. Much of what used to only exist in libraries, Yellow Pages and physical stores can now be accessed through devices that will fit in your pocket. This empowers people in developing countries to access more information and resources than most libraries can offer from the comfort of surfing the web on their smartphones. This trend has clearly driven demand for information products to skyrocket, compared with physical products.

Once you put in the initial hard work to create an information product, it is almost free to reproduce the same product over and over again. And this is especially true for digital products. Although the term might sound fancy, information product can include anything from books and blogs to videos, podcasts and newsletters.

Let me explain. When you write a book, there is a lot of hard work involved in the writing and editing (trust me, I now finally know!), and the initial fixed cost includes hiring an editor, a cover designer and, of course, your time (yes, you will see if you check my bank statement and my calendar). But once the book is ready to be published, the variable cost of printing is very low. If you produce an e-book or a video, you can essentially skip the printing step and reproduce your content at virtually no cost. Your product can be published and sold on Amazon or on your own website. It can be bought and downloaded many times without any extra input from you, generating income while you sit back, relax and reap the rewards of your hard work. The best news of all is that you probably already have the tools you need to create an information product. You can write your book in a Word document and export it as a PDF, or turn it into various e-book formats via self-publishing platforms. You can use your smartphone camera or webcam to record videos, without having to buy any fancy equipment.

Among the many information products, the most common are e-books, online courses and membership sites. But regardless of the content and format, the key principle is to turn your ideas into products that people can access and buy. Ideas in your head don't sell, but by turning those ideas into intellectual properties, they can be monetized. You might think, "I don't have anything to offer. Why would anyone listen to me?" This is simply not true. There are always people who are interested in what you have to say, but you just have to put your content in front of a suitable target audience. EvanTubeHD is a YouTube channel with more than 1.8 million subscribers and over 1.5 billion views. The mastermind behind this channel earns more than US$1 million a year. And guess what? He is only 9 years old! Evan's videos record him opening and reviewing toys, and by doing so he has built a large audience and an extremely popular YouTube channel. Everyone has something to offer, and that something can be monetized via the Internet. The key is finding your niche and building content around that niche.

One way to do so is to look at your expertise. What are the questions that people usually come to you with? What kind of advice do they usually seek from you? What are your skill sets? What can you do better than most other people? Also, look at your passion. What are the things you enjoy doing? What are the things you just won't stop talking about? Once you have decided on a topic, identify the potential ways to monetize your knowledge and ideas.

You might want to teach people a language you speak. For example, if you are interested in teaching Japanese, you can write an e-book or create a video tutorial. You can produce workbooks with exercises. You can produce a phrasebook or portable phrase cards for people visiting Japan. Or you might want to write about the local area you live in. You can produce a travel guide presenting local knowledge of what your area has to offer, reviews of interesting places to visit, what the best restaurants are, all the insider tips and perhaps suggested itineraries of how to get the most out of visiting that area.

Then, research the competition. See what your competitors are offering and think of ways you can stand out in the marketplace by creating something better or different, which can take a lot of effort and investment in order to create more superior products. A faster way to stand out is to be very specific and become a monopoly in your own niche that you just created. And to do so in a crowded marketplace, you need to target a specific audience. For example, instead of teaching everyone who wants to learn Japanese, you may choose to appeal to working professionals who want to learn Japanese. As opposed to a general audience, where you teach them merely casual Japanese phrases, you can offer bonus modules on cultural etiquettes of doing business with Japanese people and business terminologies in Japanese to tailor to your audience's needs. Moreover, by having a specific target audience, you can advertise to a very specific demographic. Instead of marketing on Facebook Ads, you might want to consider buying ads on LinkedIn to appeal to a professional audience. By narrowing your target audience, you can offer laser-targeted content through the most effective marketing channels and carve out a niche for yourself in the marketplace.

## Webinars

*Potential result:* Positive impact on sales because of the delivery format

*Input required:* Initial effort to develop and deliver webinar presentations; can be automated later

*Pre-requisite:* Software to host webinars

Webinars are basically web-based seminars and are one of the ways to repurpose your existing content to generate extra income. What live or pre-recorded webinars offer is an opportunity to attract new leads, give great content and do a sales pitch at the end, allowing you to acquire new customers in an inexpensive way. The combination of video, audio and great content gives the impression of authenticity and easily establishes rapport. You can also be creative with how you leverage webinars to achieve your business goals.

Instead of having to book an expensive conference room and organizing all the logistics for a seminar, you can schedule a webinar easily, at a time that suits you, using software such as GoToWebinar. Once you have planned your webinar, all you need to do is to create a launch through your website, newsletters and social media channels to promote the event. Because there is very little commitment involved in signing up for a webinar — there is no need to sort out travel plans, and people just need to go a website at a particular time to join your class — they are more likely to respond to your invitation. And since you are giving your time to host the course, you can price your webinar in the $100–2,000 range depending on how long it is, how much content you are giving and how much value you have added to the webinar.

A webinar is where you can give people a taster of your products, and it essentially opens the door for selling higher-ticket items. So when designing one, it is important to have a catchy title that will draw people's attention. Although the end goal of your webinar is to do a sales pitch, you also need to deliver high-quality content and engage with your participants to justify the price tag. Make sure your participants are learning and benefiting from your course. When it comes to selling your products at the end, it is much easier to convince someone who has enjoyed your course to purchase more high-quality products from you.

Of course, in any sales process, your goal is to maximize the perceived value of your products, so as to create the feeling that what you get in return is much greater than what you are about to pay. The more you can tilt the balance that way, the more likely someone will buy from you. A sales technique is to create scarcity. For example, you can create time scarcity by giving people who have joined your webinar access to an exclusive discount page, where the discount can be anywhere from 10% to 50% or even 80% off. If they don't sign up on the spot, they will lose that offer the next time they visit your website. You can also create scarcity of the product itself — for example, by creating follow-up courses or material that can be purchased only after people have attended one of you webinars. By creating scarcity, you are also telling your participants the message that they are your valued customers and that you want them to have the best, exclusive deals. Moreover, when you restrict the window where people can purchase your products, your customers have to make a decision right away: if they don't act now, they will miss out. Your sales pitch will then become a lot more convincing.

Apart from doing live webinars, you can also pre-record your webinars and reuse them multiple times, which is a powerful way to scale up your business and free up your time. Rather than selling in a one-to-one way, webinars allow you to sell to many people at once. They are one of the closest alternatives to a live seminar or presentation, where you can deliver useful content and inform your audience about your products while interacting with them and answering their questions, all at once. Webinars are a highly effective weapon in your lead generation and sales arsenals.

## Online courses

> **Potential result:** High because of the insignificant cost of product delivery

> **Input required:** One-off, initial time and financial investment to productize information; some maintenance and upgrade later

> **Pre-requisite:** Your own or others' subject matter expertise in profitable niches

Apart from e-books and webinars, which are one-off products, another profitable information product is online courses. Did you know that the online education industry is worth US$107 billion in 2015? The Internet has opened up a powerful resource for people to learn new things easily. Instead of being limited by the courses available in your local area, you can learn from anyone, anywhere in the world. Instead of having to call various providers to check the dates and times of their courses and whether they have a space for you, you can sign up for online courses instantly and take them at your own pace. Instead of going to evening courses after work and spending more time in the commute, you can schedule your learning at whenever suits you.

Online courses are one of the hottest trends in the digital age, and many universities and institutions are also moving a lot of their courses online to expand their reach to the global market. You will be surprised to know how many people will pay to learn the stuff you know. Do not underestimate how much you can offer. As long as you know about a topic more than most people around the world do and position yourself as an authority of that field, people will want to learn from you. You don't need to be the top expert; often, people are interested to know your story and how you achieved your success. Telling your story makes you an approachable, yet authoritative, figure and helps people to connect with you more easily.

It all goes back to finding your niche, knowing your passion and targeting your audience. After you create the course content, you need to find a place to host it so people can access and purchase the materials you have created. One way is to shoot a series of videos and upload them to a closed channel on YouTube. When someone buys the course, you grant them access to that channel by giving them a specific link. Another way is to upload the course to your own website and put it behind a paywall, so that only people who have registered with you can get access to the content. There are also websites such as UseFedora.com or Udemy.com that have software to help you avoid a lot of the technical set-ups and that allow you to use their platform to host your online course. Again, people can buy access to the training materials inside.

If you have already created e-books or a blog, you can consider repurposing your content and package it in the form of an online course. Of course, you will want to add more value, content and bonuses — for example, by including cheat sheets or action plans, or maybe mini tests and activities. These additional elements will increase the perceived value of your content and allow you to give your course a much higher price tag than your e-book or blog.

### Membership sites

> **Potential result:** High because of recurring payment from subscriptions and the insignificant cost of product delivery
>
> **Input required:** Initial time and financial investment to productize information; some maintenance and content upgrade later
>
> **Pre-requisite:** Your own or others' subject matter expertise in profitable niches

While information products are good ways to generate passive income, the income stream is somewhat dependent on your promotional effort and consumer behavior. For example, your e-travel guide, "The

Ultimate Guide to the Greek Islands", might bring you a burst of income during the summer holidays but have only a few purchases in off-peak travel seasons. Therefore, a good way to secure your financial freedom is to have people set up recurring payments through membership sites, where people pay a fairly small subscription fee on a monthly basis to access exclusive content. By doing so, you are essentially building a loyal audience and a steady, regular source of income.

Such an exclusive members' section can offer higher-ticket items such as practical help sheets, follow-up tutorials, other resources or even coaching services from you or your staff. A key strategy is to price your content accordingly so that people feel like they are gaining more by paying a small but ongoing subscription fee rather than a huge one-off fee. For example, you can list the prices of the individual items included in the subscription, and display a sample calculation of how much people would save by becoming a member, or you can offer discounts for longer-term subscription plans.

Another way is to get people to sign up for your newsletters for an even smaller fee to get monthly or weekly updates containing short snippets of your knowledge on a much bigger topic. Some of these can be content that you are creating on an ongoing basis, so the only way to access the most up-to-date content is by subscribing. By doing so, you are increasing the value of your subscription service, because such content cannot be bought on a one-off basis. You are also positioning yourself as an authority and building up a loyal audience, so people are happy to pay these recurring fees to access your latest work. Of course, creating these newsletters requires a slight time commitment on your part. But if you are creating content for your website anyway, most of the time you only need to repurpose such content and schedule these e-mails to create an extra avenue of income.

Mastermind groups are a powerful type of membership sites, where you as the website owner and content creator provide a platform for like-minded people to connect not only with you but also with one another. For example, if you have an online course on your website, you can create a paid platform for people to connect and ask you questions directly on forums and discussion boards. Because there is a common topic and theme connecting these people, they are more likely to benefit more from interacting with and learning from one another than if they were to just complete the course on their own, which essentially adds value to the membership you are offering. And since these people have already committed time and money to your course and to joining the group, they are more likely to contribute to the community and make it thrive. As your community grows and becomes livelier, it requires less and less active input from you. And this is why membership sites are such a good source of steady passive income.

## Sales funnel

*Potential result:* Very high because of opportunities to cross-sell, up-sell and down-sell multiple products, depending on your customers' behavior

*Input required:* High because of the time and financial investment to connect different products together programmatically

*Pre-requisite:* Products and services at various price points

I am sure we have all experienced this before. You go into a shop wanting to buy a sandwich that costs $4, but end up spending $8 when you come out. Why? You have probably paid $2 to turn the sandwich into a meal with fries and a drink, then an extra $1 to upgrade it to a large meal and, just before you were about to pull out your wallet, an extra $1 for a cookie as dessert. Even though the original sandwich cost $4, in the end you have paid an additional $4 because of all these up-sell opportunities. As you already had the intention of buying the sandwich, adding an extra dollar or two for an upgrade seemed very logical and was not a big ask.

This is essentially what a sales funnel is. It acts like an inverted pyramid, where swathes of leads enter the top of the funnel and pass you their e-mail addresses in exchange for free content. A selection of those leads will then turn into paying customers, and then gradually progress to purchase higher price-point products as they journey deeper into the funnel. Some leads and customers will inevitably drop out of the funnel later during the process of filtering and selection, and the sales funnel is a fantastic method to segment and identify your ideal and high-value customers. In Internet marketing lingo, the free or cheaper products in the beginning are called front-end products, the products that most customers can easily afford and access from your websites and advertising campaigns. Then, as they journey deeper into your sales funnel, successful Internet marketers will then present more high-ticket, back-end products, usually ranging from $200 to several thousand dollars if not more. These back-end products are the real profit-maximizing products. They are, however, usually not presented early on, because their hefty price tags would have put off potential customers too early before they can experience the value offered by the products.

If you check your e-mail inbox now, I am sure you will find plenty of e-mail threads from various vendors or Internet marketers. This usually results from a previous purchase from them or is because you have entered your name and e-mail address on their websites in exchange for some free or inexpensive gifts or content, such as a discount voucher, video series or e-book. What then tends to happen is that you will receive a constant stream of e-mails delivering high-quality, related content, deals and products, but you will also occasionally receive e-mails that sell you a product or service at a fairly low price — say, at $10. If you make the low-ticket purchase, you will then journey deeper into their sales funnel. You are likely to receive more e-mails that build up towards more products and service that the Internet marketer is trying to sell to you. The price of each product and service is likely to increase, say from $100 to $300, $1,000, $3,000 and so on. The form of interaction with the vendor or Internet marketer may also evolve as higher-ticket products are sold to you — for example, they might invite you to join their webinar or upgrade your membership. However, if you did not make any purchase along the way, you will be placed on specific e-mail sequences that are designed to deliver more value for you and loop back to sales pitches for products and services at lower price points until you are fully convinced.

This is an example of a sales funnel, and all successful entrepreneurs and Internet marketers have a very well-established one of their own. Technology has enabled a high level of sophistication in customer relationship management and marketing. If you take a certain action, the system will automatically trigger a specific sequence of e-mails to be sent to you in the future. If you don't take the pre-specified action, it will send you a different sequence of e-mails in the future. For instance, if a company is selling you a $500 product online and you choose not to opt in, then it is likely to send you to another sales sequence that gives you more content, such as a replay of that webinar, a video or an e-book, that will eventually sell you a similar product. However, if you make the purchase, it will then send you an e-mail congratulating you for taking a great step towards the results you are paying for, and you will eventually receive more e-mails about products with higher price tags.

Having your own sales funnel is a great way to sell high-ticket items and to make big sales from a small list or customer base. Let's crunch some numbers here: if you want to make $1,000,000 in a year, you can either sell 1,000,000 units at $1 each, 1,000 units at $1,000 each or 200 units at $5,000 each. Regardless of the price point, you will still need to use the same persuasion techniques, and there is not much difference between the effort it takes to get a "yes" to a $1 product and a "yes" to a $1,000 product. In fact, it is often easier to capture sales from people who can afford the high-ticket items than from penny-pinchers, and you should always make it your goal to find the high-value customers. It is obvious that you need much fewer prospective customers to say "yes" if you sell the most expensive product than if you sell the cheapest product. In this example, you will only need 200 people to say "yes" versus 1,000,000.

Therefore, selling high-ticket items can help you reach your financial goal quicker and in a simpler way than selling low-ticket items. It is all about finding where your best customers are, branding and marketing your product, and convincing them of your product's value and the results it will generate. Once you find your highest-value customers, you can then focus your attention on them, tailor their customer experience and deliver fantastic value to them, so that you are also rewarded handsomely. Remember, the 80/20 principle is definitely applicable here.

Essentially, your goal is to attract people to sign up for your free content — say, a chapter of your e-book. After reading the chapter, some people may decide to buy your book. Then, as you start sending newsletters informing about and selling additional products or services to people on your list, some will decide to enroll in your online course or become a member on your website. Most people who have reached this point probably like your content and your brand, so when you sell them a one-day seminar, some will be convinced to join. At the end of the seminar, some might like to sign up for your coaching service. So, by giving away free content initially, you are attracting people into your sales funnel and paving the way for getting future sales from the $10 e-book, the online course of $300, the one-day seminar costing $1,000 and the personal coaching worth $5,000 .

The more established and sophisticated your sales funnel is, the more money you can make out of it. Of course, this takes a lot of work. Initially, the problem is that you have to produce and deliver a large amount of content, low-ticket products, services, e-mail sequences, and sales pitches. You will need to assemble all the components into a smooth sales funnel. The best thing about online sales funnels is that you can set it up to run automatically, once you put in the hard work of creating e-mail auto-responders and follow-up sequences, videos, sales and offer pages, etc. Building a sophisticated sales funnel will take substantial time and effort, but this is what all successful Internet marketers have in common. The whole system should automatically take care of every single aspect of customer engagement for you and deliver great return on investment and time freedom to you.

### Google AdSense

*Potential result:* Medium

*Input required:* Low effort to set up; little maintenance later

*Pre-requisite:* High traffic volume and audience base

A high-traffic web business opens up unexpected yet interesting opportunities. Once you have built up an audience or a constant stream of traffic, and you have a high volume of visitors to your site and web properties, there will be companies who would want to advertise on your space, and this is another way to monetize your online real estate. The principle is exactly the same as having billboards, where those in high-traffic areas and prominent places are the most valuable. So if you have a website, blog, YouTube channel or Facebook page, your audience and subscribers mean a lot to the companies who want to tap into your customer base. By signing up to products such as Google AdSense, you can offer an ad space on your online real estate to other advertisers. For example, if you create an ad space on your recipe blog, there will be companies who will want to use that space to advertise frying pans or other kitchen utensils, because your target audience is very similar. You will then get paid by Google for offering ad space on your online real estate.

Because you get only a very small portion of the advertising spend, this might not make a big financial dent initially. But the interesting thing is that your income from Google AdSense is directly proportional to how much traffic you can drive. So as you build your audience, having Google AdSense on your web property simultaneously could be an extra way to monetize the traffic you get, thus maximizing the return on investment from every single click that comes through to your website. It might not be a lot of money initially, but as your audience grows and your traffic increases, your Google AdSense account could grow into a decent size, and your income stream from this source could become more significant. The best thing about Google AdSense is probably that there is no extra work involved, and it is essentially an extra source of income using your existing resources.

## Online survey

> *Potential result:* Up to several hundred dollars per
> market research company per month
>
> *Input required:* Manual and repetitive work
>
> *Pre-requisite:* Registration with market research and
> survey companies

This is a quirky one: taking surveys for cash. Many companies are willing to pay millions of dollars for customer research, and one of the fastest and easiest ways to do such research is to blast out surveys to the general public at scale. Some of these surveys pay participants for taking part, either in cash or in reward coupons, so the challenge here is to strategically find out which paid surveys are recruiting participants and to take as many as possible. Websites like Top10BestPaidSurveys.net in the US or other similar local websites will aggregate and register you with many of those market research companies, so that you get alerts whenever surveys are available. Of course, this requires you to actively spend time to click through the surveys, and you also need to go through a high volume of surveys to get a sizable income.

## Financial trading

*Potential result:* Very high and directly proportional to
the size of your investment capital

*Input required:* 30–60 minutes a day during weekdays,
in addition to continuous education and
research

*Pre-requisite:* As little as US$500 and a trading account
with a broker

One of the greatest empowerment that the Internet has brought is the ability to access the financial markets in the comfort of our homes. Trading the financial markets used to be an exclusive investment exercise reserved for the largest financial institutions, corporations and governmental organizations, but the Internet has significantly lowered the barrier of entry in terms of initial investment capital. Yet, the financial markets also have the potential for the highest return on investment. You can trade financial products such as foreign exchange, options, features, stocks, commodities and bonds, most of which can be accessed and managed through various brokers. A word of warning here is that it is vital to find a broker that is heavily regulated by a credible authority so that you don't lose your money.

The benefits of trading the financial markets yourself far outweigh the benefits of handing over your money to your bank, financial adviser or pension provider. Many funds' performance has been subpar over the past few years, yet they are still entitled to a management fee that can cost at least 2% of your portfolio, regardless of whether the return on investment was positive. And if the funds were profitable over a given period, the fund managers also charge a performance fee or commission cut from the profits generated. The worst aspect is that these financial products often lock up your money for a fixed period of time, and you would be charged a heavy penalty if you insist on withdrawing the money prematurely. Furthermore, because financial institutions are often investing your money and not theirs, they may not invest as prudently as your actual risk appetites allow. The Internet is truly empowering individuals by allowing you to take back control of your money.

If you know how to read the market and how to do technical and sentiment analysis, and if you keep up with financial news and form your own opinion, financial trading can be an extremely powerful way to grow your investment portfolio and financial capital as you make more money for other means. If you grow your portfolio by 6% a month, you can essentially double it by the end of the year, and the return on investment will greatly surpass the minuscule interest rates offered by a bank's savings account.

The key components to successfully trading the financial markets are to adopt a consistently profitable trading strategy and to have the correct trader's mindset. The financial markets will always give you surprises, and even the most experienced professional traders will also have lost money in their trading careers. Warren Buffet, one of the most acclaimed investment authority, also made many investment mistakes throughout his successful career, but the trick to growing your investment pot is to consistently have more winning investments than losing ones.

Hollywood tends to depict professional traders as those who take high risk, but the key to a consistently profitable trading strategy is to manage your risks so that they are as minimal as possible. And the best traders on Wall Street are actually experts at risk management. You should also learn from the professionals and know when to get in and out of the markets. For example, you can set a target price point at which you enter the market with a trade, and you can also schedule 'stop losses', which are specific price points at which you exit the market when the price drops below or goes above your pre-specified range. Once you have set these price points and various dynamic commands, your trades are essentially scheduled automatically to get in and out of the market when the conditions are right. It is very important to use stop losses to best manage your portfolio, otherwise one unexpected trade can wipe out your entire portfolio. When you price your stop loss, always risk no more than 1% of your portfolio. The reason is, when you limit your investment to that level of risk, you need to have *4,731 losing trades in a row* at 1% risk per trade for your entire trading portfolio to be wiped out. Do you think you can make at least one winning trade out of 4,731 consecutive trades? Yes, you probably can and, in fact, you most likely will.

Of course, all of this comes with a disclaimer. This book is not legally responsible for the results of your investment portfolio, as trading the financial markets comes with a proportional amount of risk, and there is the potential of losing all your initial capital if you don't know how to manage risk. While I have highlighted some general principles and pointers, financial trading is a complicated subject that requires learning. I strongly recommend that you educate yourself sufficiently before attempting to trade the markets, or you will seriously risk losing your initial capital. Online resources like The School of Pipsology section on BabyPips.com (http://www.babypips.com/school), ForexFactory.com and many brokers' internal educational materials are good starting points. You can also apply for demo accounts with brokers to practice and hone your skills before trading with real money.

## 3 - BUYING AND DECORATING YOUR PROPERTY

### Building your own website

Unsurprisingly, your website is fundamental to your online business, because it is your real estate in the online world and is a reflection of yourself and your business. I would recommend setting up two types of websites.

The first is a website about yourself, ideally with your name as the URL. This will become your personal branding page that tells people who you are, what you do, and what you have accomplished. It is where you present yourself to the world, list your awards and achievements, and attract people to do business with you. Additionally, it acts as a centralized portal where people can see all your products, your blogs, your Facebook profile or Facebook page, LinkedIn profile, Twitter page and so on. It will be a hub displaying all the different things that you want people on the Internet to know about you. Write a short biography and invest in getting a nice professional headshot photo of yourself. Be mindful of the impression you want to give: the goal is to look professional yet approachable. These elements will make your website more authentic, which means that people are more likely to want to connect with you.

The second type of website is an e-commerce site where you capture leads, display your products and services, and process payments. Ideally, the products available on your website will be related to each other to create brand congruency, and will be organized by themes and categories to make the customer journey smoother. If you have widely different categories of products, such as cosmetics and self-help e-books, then consider having a separate website for each category, because the target customers would be very different. However, it is still important to brand yourself and your company on these websites to build stronger brand recognition and credibility.

### Buying web domain

A domain name is essentially an address on the World Wide Web. When selecting your domain name, there are several rules of thumb to take into consideration. First, the domain name should not be too long so that it is easy enough for users to find you. This is important to prevent the 'fat finger' issue — in which users are more likely to make typos when typing on their small mobile device screens — especially now that web traffic from mobile devices are overtaking desktop traffic. Second, keep it simple. Since the Internet can be accessed across the globe, many of your potential visitors, customers and clients are not necessarily native English speakers. Using words that are prone to misspellings makes it extra difficult for people to get to your webpage. Avoid putting words that end and start with the same letter next to each other — for example, extreme*e*xperimentations.com. For some strange reason, people tend to type one 'e' rather than two after 'extreme', so they are likely to spell the web address incorrectly and go to the wrong website. Third, the domain name should be relevant to your product. When people type in a URL, they have certain expectations about the webpage they are about to visit. So if the website turns out to be completely irrelevant, this creates a bad first impression and user experience.

I had several clients who had bought web domains and had been driving a lot of traffic to their websites. However, there were a few occasions where I misspelled their domain names the first time I visited, which made me wondered why I kept going to error pages. Think about how many other people would have had a similar experience and how many business opportunities they would have missed as a result. I was sure I was not the only one making those common spelling errors, so I advised my clients to buy the extra domain names with the misspellings and redirect those domains to their main webpages. In some cases, my clients have successfully increased their website traffic by another 20% overnight through the extra domain names, because apparently those 20% of people never knew how to spell their original domain names.

Therefore, be careful of how you set up your domain name and think of all the potential misspellings. If a competitor buys a very similar domain name, then customers who are intending to go to your website will end up going to your competitor's site, thinking that it is your website. An example would be HowToMakeMoney.com and How2MakeMoney.com. It is wise to buy up the extra domains when you first set up your website, and redirect these additional domain names to your main website to capture all the extra traffic. With advanced web analytics software, which I'll cover later in this chapter, you will be able to see how much of your traffic is coming from these misspelled domains. If you discover that some of those additional domain names are not redirecting much traffic, you can choose not to renew the domain when it expires, so there is nothing to lose.

Finally, always buy a .com domain extension, as it is the most intuitive and universal. It is the easiest for your leads and customers to find you. A .com domain extension also implicitly enhances your website's credibility because it gives the impression that your website, and by extension your company, is global. You can of course be creative with new domain extensions, which are usually cheaper than .com at the moment. These new domain extensions, such as .london, .kiwi,

.cafe and .guru, might be particularly interesting for businesses in a certain location or for certain types of products. As your business expands, it is worth creating localized websites with specific country domain extensions, such as .co.uk and .com.au, to customize content for the local audience. However, because of the universality of .com extensions, it is advisable to have a .com website as your main one. You can choose to redirect all traffic to your .com site, or create different localized sites for each domain extension. The choice depends on the type of business, and it is always wise to test and compare the performance of your collection of websites. For many online businesses, the domain extension is also part of the brand name. For example, even though hotels.com have localized sites like hotels.cn and hotels.fr, the overarching brand is still known as "hotels.com". Therefore, if you have several domain extensions of the same website, try to be consistent with which one you use as the main brand name.

Websites from which you can buy domain names include NameCheap.com and GoDaddy.com. A credible provider will let you know instantly whether your potential domains are available. You cannot actually own a domain on the Internet; when you buy a domain name, you are renting it for at least a year, which means that it will need to be renewed before the expiry date. If you are short on ideas, business name generators can be helpful starting points: some of them will give you many suggestions on the basis of your chosen keyword, and some will give you trendier names with invented words (such as Skype and Trello). Many of these generators can be found by a simple Google search. One of my favorite is available on Shopify (http://www.shopify.com/tools/business-name-generator), which presents you only with business names that have available domains.

## Hosting your domain

Once you have a domain name, your address on the World Wide Web, you need a place to physically store the website on a server somewhere. This is what we call hosting. There are many hosting services out there, and a lot of them give you the ability to host multiple domains under one hosting account. Some hosting services also offer you domain purchase services; however, the general advice is to host your domain with a different company from the one you bought your domain from, because migrating between different hosting companies will be easier later on should you wish to do so.

Hosting costs slightly more than buying your domain, but it is one of your initial investments. Setting up an online business is a lot easier than setting up an offline one, and one of the reasons is that buying and hosting a domain is much cheaper than buying or renting a physical storefront or an office space. With hosting, don't always go for the cheapest option because you are essentially determining where your server will be based and where you are going to put your websites. You would want to find a reliable host that does not go down, so your business can be up and running 24/7. One option is to host your domain with Google using Google Apps for Work, where you can also get an e-mail account with that domain name and a few other Google products, such as data storage on Google Drive, Google Calendar, video meetings on Google Hangout, Google Docs and Google Sheets. The second option is GoDaddy.com, an excellent hosting service that has been around for a long time. Another is HostJill.com, which is also an affordable and reliable service that allows you to host an unlimited number of websites.

Once you purchase your hosting server plans, you will need to link up the URL domain that you bought from NameCheap.com or GoDaddy.com with your hosting server. That way, your website is officially live and running. The next step is to renovate and decorate your 'store front' — building and designing the website.

## Building your website with WordPress

Now that you have bought 'land' in the online world, you can start to build your 'house'! You can get a professionally designed website that costs anything from US$100 to US$5,000, or you can do it for free (or for a small fee) via WordPress. It is a plug-in supported by most hosting services that you can download onto your website. WordPress has a collection of website templates with a wide range of themes and designs. These templates will provide a basic layout for your website, where you can create different pages, customize the content, adjust the font and so on. WordPress' interface is so easy to use that most people can and will learn it in under half an hour. And once you learn how to use the core features, you can get your website up and running in no time.

It is a common misconception that you need to have a very professionally designed website to be able to do well and convert lots of visitors into customers. This is simply not true. There are many profitable websites out there that are clunky and look outdated. Look at Yahoo, Craigslist, Gumtree and even MSN.com. These websites still follow the old-fashioned way of throwing an overwhelming amount of links and content on the homepage. And yet they are still popular, well known and profitable. Many websites nowadays tend to have a minimalist, clean and neat design, which is more aesthetically pleasing and perfectly doable with WordPress.

In fact, WordPress powers 1 in 6 websites on the Internet, but most people do not realize this because it is very versatile. For an online business, the most important thing is to make sure your website, and everything around it (say, your business profiles on various social media platforms), is extremely convincing and persuasive to maximize sales. Here, the key is to think like an online marketer rather than a web designer. Although it is important that your website is aesthetically appealing, the ultimate goal is to optimize your web business such that it gives a pleasant user experience, provides the most value to users, attracts a large number of potential customers and converts a large proportion of those leads into sales.

One of the great things about WordPress is that it can be both a blog and a website at the same time, so you present content that is more static, such as your sales page and perhaps some videos and images, on the website part, while constantly updating and engaging with users on the blog section. One key functionality that WordPress offers is the ability to create hidden pages, the access of which is limited to registered users with login details. This way, you can create a membership site to offer exclusive products and content to registered users. You don't need to know HTML or any other coding language at all to use most of the functionalities, and you don't need to be a web designer to have a nice-looking and fully functional website. WordPress has all the basic functionalities you will need.

## Designing your website

In the digital economy, most businesses do not have issues in generating volume and scale. The problem is usually not getting the fundamentals correct and then suffering the consequences later. I therefore urge you to make sure that your business's basics are superb before scaling up. Finding traffic is easy, especially with some marketing dollars, but building a sustainable business model takes more solid effort. In fact, there is so much traffic on the Internet and the number of users is still rapidly growing globally. The numbers are mind-blowing. In August 2015, Facebook even celebrated 1 billion users in a single day!

In view of this, it is important to bear in mind the concept of a "lean start-up", where you start something small, test it out and prove the concept, before rolling out onto a bigger scale. The same principle also applies to everything you do with website design. Start building your website with WordPress, which offers a range of free customizable themes and templates that dramatically change the look and feel of your website. Again, the 80/20 principle applies here: much of website design is about achieving the 20% that will give you the 80% of results. Yes, presentation is important, but it is about finding the right elements to focus on. Once you find the 20% of inputs that add real value, just rinse and repeat them and you should expect incredible results in a highly leveraged manner.

I am sure we have all been to poorly done websites that are difficult to navigate, that have unclear information and that look unappealing. As I said earlier, your website is like your physical store, and your ultimate goal is to provide a pleasant customer journey. A key concept here is to always think in the perspective of a customer. If they visit your website, how would they feel? And what could you do so that they can experience your website in the best possible way?

You would want your visitors to enjoy browsing your website, find the information they need in a clear format, without being redirected through too many irrelevant pages, and not get bombarded with too much information. You would want to pick a color scheme that evokes the right emotions. It is often a good idea to have a video at the start of the customer journey and design your website like an IKEA store, with a clearly designated path to guide visitors through the whole experience.

At the same time, you don't want to create any unpleasant experience or annoyance. Always visually guide the customer towards where they should click next and how they should explore the content on your website, and eventually to the payment page where they can buy your products. Having a clear menu of options is also helpful to let the visitor pick and choose where they want to go. All of these basic website design principles are highly applicable to the selling of both physical and digital products.

Having these basic elements in place will most probably give you the 80% of results. However, if you want to achieve something more, websites such as fiverr.com, Elance.com and 99designs.com are where you can get graphic or web designers to improve the look of your website. I will cover fiverr.com in more detail in Chapter 7, but it is essentially a marketplace where freelancers post jobs at a flat rate of US$5 per task, with the content of each task defined by the freelancers themselves. Alternatively, you can hire a professional web designer to work for you. The most important point here is that you should slowly ramp up your website depending on your risk appetite and your budget. You really don't have to start that big. You're not building the next Google just yet: it could become the next Google, but it will take some time from now. And bear in mind how Google looked when it first started. It was completely different to how it looks now, and its many features and product lines were introduced and optimized gradually over time. Just remember this: "the journey of a thousand miles begins with one step" (Lao Tzu, ancient Chinese philosopher).

Another important thing to consider is the conversion rate, which is the percentage of users who take a desired action — for example, the percentage of visitors to a website who make a purchase. Some of the best-looking websites might not be the ones with the highest conversion. So be careful every time you launch a brand-new look and feel to your website. Measure the impact on conversion rate. Test it out to see whether it is leading to more sales and look at the web analytics metrics to see how well your website is doing. While paying $5,000 for a professionally designed website will give you something that looks fantastic, it does not necessarily guarantee a higher conversion rate and more business. Ultimately, you need to optimize your website to generate more traffic and attract more customers. So, remember, start with the basics and then work your way up, keeping track of your website's performance along the way to build the website that works best for you and your business.

## Processing payments

To generate income via your website, it has to be able to process payments, and there are several ways to do so. A common way is to set up a merchant account at the bank. You will have to fill in some paperwork to set up the account officially, so that you can process credit or debit card payments, as well as PayPal payments, bank transfers and other forms of payment.

Another way is to set up a PayPal business account, where PayPal does most of the software development and the coding for you. All you have to do is copy and paste the button onto your website, and it will be ready to process payments. Obviously, you will have to verify your bank payment details with PayPal so that the money gets deposited into your PayPal account, and you always have the option of taking the money out whenever you need to. In essence, PayPal becomes your merchant account.

Look around and consider these options. Many of the world's biggest businesses use PayPal as their payment system, and it is also my personal favorite. It has a very user-friendly interface, and is reliable and trustworthy.

## Creating sales and offer pages

Once the skeleton of your website is ready, focus on creating your sales and product offer page. As its name suggests, it is the page where you sell your product and present its features with descriptions, pictures, videos and so on. Your goal is to enhance the perception of your product, convince people of its value and benefits, and persuade your visitors into becoming your customers.

Online businesses naturally comes with a lot of metrics and numbers, which can be quite daunting at first, and it is important to know your numbers in order to truly scale up your operations. Conversion rate is one of the most useful and crucial metrics to grow your online business. It is an easily measurable metric that gives you a useful indication of your website's performance. If you can improve the conversion rate, even by just a little, all the traffic you drive to your website will have a much bigger impact on your end results. With a high conversion rate, even a low traffic volume can still generate healthy revenue and profits for you.

With this in mind, the key to creating your sales page is to optimize the conversion rate, so that more of your visitors become your customers. Some things you may want to include in your sales page are product feature, the benefits that your product is promising to deliver and the format of the product (for example, digital versus physical). Talk about what people who have used your product think of it and the results they have achieved in the form of testimonials. Promote your credibility and tell people why you are in a good position to teach them about certain things, why you are an authority in your field, why they should buy your product, what is so fantastic about your product, and what is so outstanding about you.

There are several ways to format your sales page. One is to sell your product over a video and present the entire pitch, including the product benefits, feature, price and so on, with a purchase button below to redirect to the payment page. Or you could write a sales copy to present the product in textual form, and it is often useful to include images so people will have a more concrete idea of what you are talking about. If the description is long, you can have multiple links either embedded throughout the text or in floating boxes on the side, where people can purchase straightaway if they are convinced before they reach the bottom of the page. Another way is to create a testimonial-heavy page, which is often convincing because it is social proof that your product can deliver great results.

In my opinion, the best is to have a combination of all three, so you can tailor your sales pages for specific products and to a wider range of audience. Some people may prefer reading textual description on their own and not be sold to directly. Some people may be more easily convinced by testimonials and product reviews. And still others may be more willing to receive information in the form of videos, which can give a more authentic feel.

You can also add fancy features such as an on-site live chat and customer support service, comment boxes for people to interact with you or a contact page where they can reach you directly for more information. It is sometimes useful to have a frequently asked questions (FAQ) section, where you can provide more details of your product and address some of the common doubts in a more convincing way. The key here is to try and tick all the boxes and cover all the possible scenarios. Most importantly, don't forget to include a button that leads to the payment page, where your customers can input their credit card details and purchase your product.

Pricing is a crucial determinant of the success of your business. The two main components of pricing are the actual price and the displayed price. The first way to determine your price is to add the desired profit margin on top of the total cost (i.e. the fixed and variable costs). This old-school method can risk undervaluing your products. Although many digital products have very low fixed and variable costs, selling an e-book at a regular price of US$1 would massively undervalue its worth. Another way to set your price is to base your decision on the price of your competitors. This is not a bad way to start and can help you gauge market demands. But because pricing is a key lever in your business, don't always go for the market rate. Doing so would not allow enough differentiation between you and your competitors, and you would not be able to efficiently capture high-value customers who are willing to pay more. Finally, you can price your products on the basis of the value you provide to your customers.

Your ultimate goal in pricing is to increase the actual and perceived value, and suppress the actual and perceived cost. From a user's perspective, the buying decision is often not about the absolute dollar amount but instead about the perceived value. You can increase the value-to-cost ratio by giving away bonuses and offering follow-up services, or by decreasing the price. However, think carefully about the earlier point I made about your price in relation to your competitors'. Set a price that differentiates and positions you highly, and beware of cutting the price so much so that it down-brands your business and downplays the value of your products and services. Furthermore, the price point is a signal about your product's value and position in the marketplace. For example, Apple's Macintosh computers are always priced near the upper end of the market and are significantly more expensive than most PCs with similar specifications, but there is nevertheless a lot of demand for these high-end computers.

Price presentation includes plenty of components that play on the consumer psychology, and getting this right is crucial for your business. Daniel Kahneman and Amos Tversky's Prospect Theory proposes that, in consumer behavior, the feeling of loss is greater than the feeling of gain. For example, people often prefer ordering set menus than a-la-carte even though the final price might be similar. The action of paying for three separate courses involves three purchasing decisions, and this feeling of loss (i.e. giving away money) is greater than that when paying one bigger sum once for a three-course set menu, and it usually outweighs the feeling of gain (i.e. having more choices from the a-la-carte menu). Therefore, the aim of price presentation is to reinforce the idea that the value you are offering is much higher than the cost they are paying.

You can present your price as an absolute dollar figure, a percentage discount or a coupon code. If tax (and shipping) are excluded, the displayed price will be lower, but this might create an unpleasant experience at checkout when the customer has to pay a higher final price than expected. The size of the displayed price, where it is shown on the webpage, when it is revealed in a video pitch and the language used will also affect consumer psychology. There is no magic pricing strategy because so much depends on the target customers and the type of products. Therefore, my advice is to always test out different pricing approaches and find the one that suits your business best.

Another useful way to increase conversion rate is to present the concept of scarcity, whether it is scarcity by time or quantity. An example is to have a time-limited offer — say, "If you purchase this item in the next 24 hours, you can get it for an early-bird price." Or to include certain perks and bonuses for the first customers — for example, "Free bonus one-to-one coaching if you are the first 10 customers." Just be careful that when you present a scenario of scarcity, you actually *need* to make that scarcity happen. When you say that a certain offer is going to expire in the next 24 hours, you will need to lock people out of the offer or change the price back to the original after the specified time. This is important because it preserves your credibility and ensures that integrity is associated with your brand.

Ultimately, what works is a combination. But always, always remember to test what works well for your website and what does not. This is the beauty of having an online business — you can instantly change the look of your website, as well as the text, videos and images, at a very low, or almost no, cost. Compare this with an offline store, where a lot of time and money will need to be invested to renovate the storefront, launch a new product line and create promotional material. In the online world, however, new products can be launched almost instantly, and the performance of your website can be measured easily and quantitatively using a wide range of metrics in real time, allowing you to analyze which components work best and which features give the highest conversion rate.

## Branding

To effectively sell products and services on the Internet, it is very important to develop credibility and social proof, and to up-brand yourself so that people have a good impression of you, your products and your business, and therefore trust what you say and what your products deliver. Branding underpins the whole customer experience from the moment someone lands on your homepage to after they have purchased your products.

A big part of branding is building and maintaining a good reputation, and there are three key elements here: clarity, credibility and consistency. Make it clear what you stand for and why you are credible. Think of ways to wow people and make yourself stand out: do you have a qualification from a prestigious institution? Do you have any outstanding achievements or have you won any awards? Do you have any life experiences that make you unique? Have you done anything to give back to society? Have you been invited to give speeches? Have you had any high-profile clients before? All of these will position you as an authority. Ideally, you would brand yourself as someone who not only has the knowledge on a certain topic but also has the experience. Not only have you done your research, but you have also put what you preach into practice and have helped other people. This is why testimonials and positive reviews are so valuable in branding.

The marketplace is crowded nowadays, but the good news is, you don't have to be the world's number-one expert on a particular topic to succeed. It is not always the number one who gets all the business, but you need to find a way to stand out and brand yourself in that angle. This is why it is important to create your own niche and find your target audience. It is much easier to become established within a niche than to compete with the big names and big corporations in a big field. Creating a niche is one of the ways to up-brand yourself. In fact, the more specific your customer base is, the easier it is to target because you will know exactly what your customers like and dislike. You will essentially become number one within this niche and can monopolize it. This will also enhance your authority and open up more business opportunities.

If you are able to brand yourself well, you have a chance of dominating a crowded marketplace and can also acquire more customers and business partners, because people will have heard of your name or brand through word of mouth and testimonials, and will be more likely to reach out to you. Good branding can save you a lot of money on traffic generation, since more people will search directly for your brand or go directly to your website. These people are also more likely to become purchasing customers, as it is much easier to convince someone who already has a good impression of your brand than someone who knows nothing about your business.

Branding and credibility extend to the entire customer journey. Even if people have heard of your business, if your website presents the wrong impression or is inconsistent with what your brand stands for, their perception of your brand will be affected. Negative comments or reviews on social media, blogs and forums will also down-brand you and hinder your credibility.

Finally, inconsistency within your brand — for example, if what you present on the sales page is not what you promise on the homepage, or if your sales page has a very different message from the rest of your website — is detrimental to your business. When it comes to purchasing, most people tend to find reasons not to buy from you. Don't give them that reason. If you pride yourself in good customer service, then make sure you do deliver what you have promised. John Maxwell, the leadership expert, once wrote "the more followers see and hear their leader being consistent in action and word, the greater their consistency and loyalty. *What they hear, they understand. What they see, they believe!*" Inconsistency within your brand will create a bad impression and damage the reputation of you and your business, so always make sure your brand is clear, credible and consistent.

## Optimizing with web analytics software

As I mentioned earlier, your website is essentially a storefront on the Internet. Therefore, a key to success is to optimize the customer journey, because how people experience your website will directly determine the conversion rate. How users interact with your website and behave on the website will affect whether they are going to purchase your product in the end. Hence, it is crucial to optimize your website along each step and element of the user experience.

When people land on your homepage, is it clear what the website is about? When they click on one button, is it intuitive where they are going next, and does this align with their expectations? Design your website as if you are designing a physical store, and pay attention to how the customer journey should look like. For example, you can color-code certain buttons to make them more eye-catching and serve as a visual guide. The user flow should also be logical and smooth. A healthy balance between the text, videos and images should help too. There is always room to improve how users experience and interact with different aspects of your website.

However, a sophisticated Internet marketer will measure various metrics through web analytics software to find out exactly which areas need improvement. The beauty of online marketing is that everything can be quantified and recorded: by analyzing the large amount of data collected, you can optimize your website and test out various features. Web analytics will tell you how long users spent on a particular page, where they came from before they landed on that page, where they went after that page, and the percentage of people who clicked on a particular link out of everyone who landed on that page. It can also tell you the marketing channel from which your visitors came, so you can assess whether your marketing strategies worked.

All of these metrics can be measured through software such as Omniture or Google Analytics, and it is very important to learn about these metrics, understand what they mean for your website and your business, and to know how to analyze them. To become a more sophisticated Internet marketer, you will need to start engaging in this kind of data-driven approach when optimizing your website and, ultimately, your conversion rate. Say, out of 1,000 people who visited your website, 20 went on to purchase your product, your conversion rate is 2%. If you are able to optimize the shopping experience and sales page so that 30 more people out of that 1,000 end up buying your product, you will have more than doubled your conversion rate to 5%. Small increases in conversion rate can bring about exponentially profitable gains.

Being able to measure different components with web analytics software is only a starting point. With all these data comes the opportunity to test the performance of any feature, page, product, service and even color scheme when you launch them on your website. Instead of guessing blindly what features will boost your conversion rate, you can research best practices of your direct competitors and other industries, read up on industry blogs and articles, and finally experiment yourself. Taking a data-driven, hypothesis-driven approach is key here. Do not let you gut instinct affect your decisions, especially when the data is statistically significant. When just starting out, however, the dataset is probably quite small from the low traffic volume. You should then, in that case, put yourself in the customers' shoes and think about what a smooth user experience should look like. Feel free to get your friends or even get me to have a look at your website! Moreover, you can make sure that the new feature is not damaging the conversion rate you have built up previously. As you can launch various features instantly and get data in real time, you have much more flexibility in creating online products than offline products. You can even take more risks, because if something doesn't work, you can always stop it and revert to the previous.

There are three main ways to test. The first is split testing, or what is called "A/B testing". Here, you randomly split the traffic to version A and version B of your website and see which one performs better. If you want to add a background image to your homepage, version A would be your original homepage without the image, and version B would be the new homepage with the image. When you do split testing, always change one variable at a time and try to control for other factors as much as possible. For example, rather than directing all UK customers to version A and foreign customers to version B, it would be fairer to split the UK segment randomly, and direct 50% to A and 50% to B. This way, you can compare between two groups with similar or identical behavior. If version B, the new version with the background image, proves to have better key performance indicators — for example, higher conversion rate, higher click-through rate (the percentage of people who click on the link to your website out of all who see your website on the search results page) and lower bounce rate (the percentage of visitors who leave the website after only browsing one page) — then you may want to consider switching over. If not, hypothesize another potential improvement, design that feature and test it out again.

Additionally, the more granular your test segment, the more precise your analysis can be. So instead of looking at traffic from the UK as one segment, you can selectively look at London. Or even within London, you can test how one area performs differently from another. Beware of drawing important conclusions based on overall averages without taking potential biases into account.

The second is multivariate testing, in which multiple versions of your website are tested at the same time. But again, you can only segment your traffic in various chunks if you have large traffic volumes. Otherwise, each variant or traffic segment will end up with insufficient data for you to confidently draw a conclusion and make a decision.

The third way to test would be to do a time series. This is especially applicable when you are changing a setting on your website and when it is difficult to split the traffic into segments. Say, you want to change the payment method from your own bank's merchant account to your PayPal account. You may want to test how the different payment options affects people's purchasing behavior and how many people drop out at each of the payment stage, or whether one provider makes it easier for your customers to go through the transaction stages. This is the kind of change that is difficult to do a split test, because it essentially changes the entire website. You can still do a split test by having two versions of your website, one with your bank's merchant account and one with your PayPal account, but this will require a lot more work to maintain both accounts and versions. However, if you do a time-series test, you can measure your website's performance before and after the change, with that change isolated. With all else being equal, what is the impact of that one change you have made? The problem, of course, is that it is difficult to account for seasonality and for other changes in traffic or on the website during the pre-test and post-test time periods. But you should try your best to keep all other things equal, like length of both test periods, mix of traffic and website appearance.

With every change you implement on your website, always ensure that it is optimizing the performance of your business rather than damaging what you have built. This is why web analytics is such a powerful tool:

when everything can be measured and data can be analyzed, there is no guessing game involved, and you will have a much higher rate of success than if you were to rely on your intuition alone.

## Optimizing for mobile devices

Mobile devices are rapidly overtaking the use of traditional PC or Macintosh desktops and laptops. Mobile traffic has started to exceed desktop traffic in many countries, especially as developing countries catch up with digital innovations and adopt new technologies. In these countries, many people are bypassing the desktop generation and going straight to mobile devices because they are typically more affordable. As a result, many more people are browsing websites on mobile devices. These, of course, include smart phones and tablets of various sizes, with several thousand different screen dimensions, produced by manufacturers around the world. Therefore, your website and products will be viewed on devices with slightly different dimensions, and user behavior, of course, changes accordingly.

When you surf the Internet on your phone, you will notice that many websites, especially the more traditional ones, are not designed for mobile devices. A lot of information is displayed on the screen, but in a much smaller font that you can barely see. Because you need to zoom in and out with your fingers to see the different parts of a website, these non-mobile-optimized websites are much more difficult to navigate and much less user friendly. By contrast, mobile-optimized websites look more like an app, with text and pictures in the right size to fit the dimensions of your screen. On Google, instead of having a wide webpage with pictures and two columns of text ads, all the text ads are lined up in one single column to fit the slimmer width of mobile devices.

Therefore, optimizing your website for mobile devices can improve the user experience. It is slightly more difficult to do so on your own and may require some investment in hiring a web designer, but it is something you definitely should consider bringing into your mix. Having a mobile-optimized website where users don't have to zoom in and out to view your content and where the buttons are much bigger makes your website more intuitive and easy to use. Moreover, by adopting a responsive design, your mobile-optimized website can dynamically adjust itself to different screen dimensions, so that irrespective of the mobile device your visitors use, they can have a great experience. Of course, this is getting into the more technical side of things, and you have to assess at which phase of your website and which stage in your online marketing journey do you want to invest in optimizing your website for mobile devices.

Although having a website will allow people to find you through a Google search or other social media channels, mobile apps are another marketing channel that is becoming more and more prominent. Once downloaded, your app is always visible on people's devices. It allows your customers to access your product and content at their fingertips by clicking one button only, instead of having to launch a web browser and finding their way to your website. Your app is a direct marketing channel to your customers: you can use it to provide general information, news feeds, search features, user accounts and so on depending on the nature of your business, as well as to send push notifications from time to time. Because apps are interactive, you can keep your customers engaged, and it is a good way to build brand recognition and loyalty. You can develop your own app using software such as Como, BuildFire or AppsBuilder; alternatively, you can get someone to program and create a prototype for you, although this will require more investment.

With web analytics software, you can measure and assess how much mobile traffic you are getting. If it constitutes a large proportion of your website's overall traffic, and if you see a demand for a mobile app, then you should consider adding an app to your range of products. Always evaluate whether such a move will make sense financially and will bring a healthy return on investment. Of course, the focus is always on the quality of your products and content of your website: get the basics right, and you can easily scale up and roll out other features.

## 4 - THROWING YOUR HOUSEWARMING PARTY ON A SHOESTRING

### Acquiring free traffic to your website

When you open a store in the offline world, you will want to make sure that it is located in a busy commercial district, on the busiest streets in the city center. Those would be the most expensive, prime location because it is almost guaranteed that people will be eyeballing your logo, looking at the window display and coming in to find out what your store has to offer. This is only the start of the customer experience: once they are attracted and step into your store, they will start browsing your products and chatting to you or your staff. If you opened the store in the middle of nowhere or in a corner tucked away in the basement of a mall, where people are unlikely to pass by, then no matter how beautiful your store is and how good your products are, you will not be able to thrive as a business.

The same thing happens in the online world. Even with the most professionally done website and the best products, if you don't know how to drive traffic to your website, then it is almost impossible to generate income and grow your business. Even if you are not trying to make money just yet, you will still want people to read what you have just posted on your blog.

In the online world, there are two types of traffic: free and paid. Free traffic is when people visit your website without you paying a penny for it — for example, when they are introduced to your website through word of mouth, social media posts or a link in an e-mail. More frequently, people will visit your website when it shows up in search results. Say, someone searched for "how to lose five kilos in two days" on Google. If the various components on your website and about your website elsewhere online happen to be relevant to this search query, then Google will rank you fairly high up in the search results. And that person is likely to click on the link and be redirected to your fitness website. This is essentially a free click-through visit and is an extremely important source of traffic when you are starting out, unless you have deep pockets already. Of course, this is not as easy as it sounds. Because it is free, there is no guarantee that you will always be ranked near the top.

Alternatively, if you have the budget to fund a marketing campaign, you can pay for a guaranteed stream of traffic by advertising on other high-traffic media platforms, such as Google and its Display Network, YouTube, Facebook and other social media sites. Apart from buying good ranking in search results when someone searches for a particular keyword, you can also buy banner ads and sponsored tweets. By occupying the 'prime real estate' on those platforms, paid advertising is the best way to exponentially scale up your business. It is doable even without too much money: with online marketing campaigns, you can set precise daily or monthly budgets to make sure you will not overspend. I will cover the various bidding and payment models in more detail in the next chapter. However, because you are investing money into these paid marketing channels, it is essential to make sure that all components of your website (for example, design, sales page, payment processor and ideally the sales funnel as well) are functional and ready for business.

### E-mail marketing and list building

*Potential result:* Extremely high potential return on investment because of the ability to communicate for free to people who gave you permission to e-mail them

*Input required:* Continuous effort to drive traffic to your lead-capture pages and to communicate to your e-mail marketing audience

*Pre-requisite:* E-mail marketing software and lead-capture software

One of the most important concepts in online marketing is list building, which is when you generate a base group of potential or existing customers around a specific niche or topic, who are interested in the area or have purchased related products before. Faced with a choice between US$10 million and a large e-mail list, most Internet marketers would choose the e-mail list. Why? As the saying goes, "the money is in the list". Whereas the $10 million is static if you don't grow it and will deplete once you start spending it, an e-mail list is the key to generating a lot of money online at minimal costs and efforts. Having a list allows you to reach out to a group of potential customers easily. All you need to do is to send a mass e-mail with promotional content or a newsletter containing updates on your website to draw people's attention.

Think of it as throwing a big party and sending invitations to all your friends. Not everyone will show up, but some will, and those who come are usually your closest friends and the people who matter to you most. In the same way, imagine sending a mass e-mail about a product launch. Let's assume only one out of the 100 people will buy your product at $100. This may not sound like a lot, but imagine if your list has 100,000 people. Even if only 1% of them end up buying a $100 product from you, you will make $100,000 just from sending out one e-mail! This is exactly why the money is in the list.

Having a list is crucial for three reasons. First, people on your list are different from those captured from other marketing channels. Because they have expressed interest in your products or have purchased from you before, they are more likely to be keen to read about what you have to offer and to buy from you. They are your most valuable prospects and your prime audience. Second, by delivering high-quality content consistently, you are building up your authority in the area and a relationship with your subscribers. They would regard you as someone who they can trust and connect with. Say, if you have established yourself as a fitness coach and have consistently delivered high-quality fitness tips in your e-mails, then when your subscribers want to find out more, they are more likely to go to your website than your competitors', simply because they are already familiar with your brand and know they can trust you to provide high-quality content. Third, the law of reciprocity is at work here: when you give a lot of value to your subscribers, they would feel a psychological urge to reciprocate the action and are therefore more likely to consider buying a product from you.

Contrast this with acquiring customers through search engine marketing (paid) or search engine optimization (free). The purpose of both of those is to acquire new customers by ensuring that your website occupies a favorable position in search results, the former bidding for keywords and the latter by optimizing your website. Although they are useful ways to acquire traffic to your website, as I will discuss later, optimization of marketing campaigns and your website requires a lot more financial and time investment, and not every potential lead will convert and purchase from you.

As it is not easy to acquire new customers, your goal is to add every visitor to your website to your list, so that you don't have to pay more money or invest more effort to capture the exact same customers. By adding them to your e-mail list and your customer relationship management system, you can reach out to these customers at almost no cost, and most of the revenue that results will be pure profit. Ideally, the visitors you capture from paid advertising, search engine optimization or other marketing channels are those who are visiting your site for the first time, and everyone who has visited your site will become your subscribers. Effectively, you are not actively marketing to your subscribers anymore but are instead managing customer relationships.

So, what is the best way to build up an e-mail list? Remember those pop-up boxes or landing pages that ask for your e-mail address when you visit a website? Those are what we call opt-in pages (also called squeeze pages), and they are one of the key functionalities on your website. They can also appear at the top or on one side in a fairly visible section. The purpose of an opt-in page is to convince your visitors to provide their e-mail addresses — one of the most valuable pieces of personal data you can obtain from your potential customers — so that you can reach out to them directly.

But of course, if you don't have enough incentive, why would people voluntarily give up their e-mail addresses? This is exactly why you need to offer something for free in exchange for such valuable information. This could be a sample chapter of an e-book, a video, a complimentary consultation, a free trial of a training course or an exclusive deal. By offering something for free, even people who may not be buying your products right away can experience what you have to offer without any financial commitment. You should aim to make it a no-brainer for your leads to input their e-mail addresses. After you have added them to your e-mail list, you can keep them engaged and informed about your latest products, as well as push them deeper into the sales funnel. They are more likely to buy from you as the customer relationship develops. This is why it is so important to turn your captured traffic into your e-mail list. E-mail marketing is, by far, one of the most cost-effective customer relationship management and sales approaches, and it is most likely to give you the highest return on investment.

WordPress has a few plug-ins that allow you to create opt-in pages. More professional software such as LeadPages, which charges a small fee per month, offers plug-and-play templates and A/B split testing features to help you better optimize your opt-in page. This page can either be a pop-up on your site or be prominently displayed on your homepage. Test which layout, color and size work best for your product, website and customers. Make sure your opt-in page is convincing enough that your visitors will willingly input their e-mail addresses. Be clear about what the free gifts are and ensure that they are suitable and attractive to your target audience.

However, there are a few words of caution here. First, it is important to strike a balance. Be careful not to make the squeeze page too annoying for your visitors because they would otherwise bounce out of the page. For example, some websites force users to input their e-mail addresses or like their Facebook page before they can browse any content. The worst part is that some of those websites even adopt a slightly condescending tonality and state that the 'free gift' is simply the "permission to browse content on the website". Not much of an attractive incentive, really. Other examples are opt-in boxes that consistently appear or even follow the mouse cursor until the users input their e-mail addresses.

Second, do not spam your users, as this creates annoyance and inconvenience. In fact, many e-mail marketing software will ban your account if many of your users mark you as spam or unsubscribe from your list. Third, make sure you keep your subscribers' e-mail addresses private and confidential. Although many people are willing to pay big money to buy your customer data, you are throwing away your reputation and trust when you agree to seal such a deal. Your subscribers have voluntarily given their e-mail addresses to you — and only to you. Even when you are doing joint venture partnerships, do not share your list with your partners; rather, maintain control over your list and send e-mails yourself on behalf of your partners. Finally, be ethical with the content and sales pitches included in your e-mails. Do not underestimate the reach of your e-mails and the influence you have over your subscribers.

### Search engine optimization and content marketing

*Potential result:* Free, qualified traffic from search engines

*Input required:* Continuous investment in building and optimizing content

*Pre-requisite:* Online presence on many high-quality sites

As I mentioned earlier, the biggest source of free traffic is via search engines, of which the best and largest is indisputably Google. Here are some shocking statistics: Google currently processes 40,000 search queries every second on average, which translates to more than 3.5 billion searches per day and 1.2 trillion searches per year worldwide. YouTube, which is also owned by Google, is the second largest search engine. It has more than 1 billion users, with 300 hours of video being uploaded every minute. Unthinkable before the age of YouTube, people nowadays prefer a video response to their queries. Let's say someone is searching for "how to make sushi", instead of reading recipe after recipe online, it is a much more engaging experience to watch someone, perhaps a celebrity chef, presenting a step-by-step demonstration on how they prepare a delicious meal.

To leverage the huge source of potential traffic that search engines can provide, you need to optimize everything you do online on the basis of what search engines 'prefer'. Relevance is perhaps the most important factor search engines care about. Google and other search engines know that when users find relevant answers quickly on their search results, they will keep returning to those search engines next time they need answers. Generally, the more relevant your websites and online presence are to the users' search queries, the higher up you will rank in the search results, and the more favorable the display format is. Your website's position in search results is very important, because very few people click on links appearing in lower positions on the first page or even go to later pages at all.

Therefore, search engine optimization (SEO) becomes the key tactic to drive free traffic from search engines to your website. In the past, Internet marketers have tried numerous dark tactics to trick Google's 'spider', which 'crawls' the Internet to index (i.e. to take a snapshot of) webpages into its database. Some of these tactics include inputting the same keywords into the tag multiple times, or putting in hidden keywords all over their website in the same font color as the background to enhance their apparent relevance. But since then, search engines' anti-spam departments have continuously tackled these sneaky tactics, and it is now fairly difficult to game the system. These anti-spam efforts will only intensify in the future, and search engines now heavily penalize spam and sneaky SEO tactics by pushing those webpages to very low rankings on its search results pages. Furthermore, Google also has a tendency to completely revamp its algorithm from time to time, and it is costly to keep up with using those dirty tactics.

Instead, the more sustainable approach is to ensure that your content is highly relevant to the niche you are targeting, and to strategically and lightly sprinkle keywords throughout your content. Then, no matter how search engines' policies change, your high-quality pages will always have a good chance of ranking better than others in search results. Make sure you also put relevant keywords into your pages' title tag, which is the name of your webpage and the title that Google's spider will index onto its search results page. Your website should also be 'Google spider-friendly' by ensuring that the website's architecture and structure are as logical and clean as possible. Seek professional help for this, as it is slightly more technical.

There are two types of SEO: on page and off page. On-page SEO means optimizing your actual website to contain the relevant keywords, so that when someone searches for those keywords, Google will quickly index your website and give it a high ranking in the search results on the basis of relevance. This is why you should be extremely strategic about the keywords you target. If you try to target every single keyword, your content will be very keyword-rich for multiple keywords but diluted. Your website may not rank near the top for any keyword, but merely average ranks for numerous search queries. As I mentioned above, also be careful not to create spam because you will be penalized otherwise. Once Google identifies your website as spam, it will push it all the way down in the search results, where it is very unlikely to be found by anyone.

In addition to the quality of your website's content, search engines also judge the relevance of your website by how popular it is and how relevant it is to other people on the Internet. Are people blogging about your website? Do your products get mentioned and commented on social media? Off-page SEO is all about having a lot of high-quality links that redirect back to your website. If your pages are mentioned on reputable sites, those links will be deemed higher quality. Conversely, if your website is constantly being mentioned on scam prevention websites or receives negative comments on forums and discussion boards, then these are considered negative user-generated content and may count against your site. Search engines are getting more sophisticated and can increasingly assess whether such content reflects positively or negatively of your business or website. For example, these algorithms can scan for words that signify poor content, such as "scam", "fraud" and "poor customer experience", and may penalize you as a result. Although many natural language processing tools do not perform well at detecting sarcasm and these algorithms are by no means perfect now, they will only improve in the future and be increasingly capable of detecting poor, negative content about your site. To track and measure your SEO performances, you can use Google Search Consoles, Google Webmaster Tools and other external software.

Therefore, this leads back the importance of creating high-quality content. Be careful about what you post on your website and social media platforms, and maintain your online presence wisely. If you have a YouTube channel or a Facebook page, interact with your audience to create more buzz, so that people become more aware of your products and talk about them on their own pages as well, thus generating links back to your website. When this happens, the search engines will categorize your website as popular and therefore relevant, and will display it in a higher position on search results pages. Again, as search engines become more sophisticated, websites that try to trick the search engines get penalized. Rather than relying on software that automatically generates thousands of low-quality links to your website, the goal is to create high-quality content to bring traffic to your website and ensure that all your social media platforms and affiliated channels are rich in relevant content, since this is the only way to guarantee long-term success of your SEO efforts.

This brings us to a discussion about content marketing, which is marketing by providing high-quality content on your website and on your various social media platforms, whether it is in the form of a blog post, a picture or a video. Having great content on your website is really what makes the overall customer experience engaging. High-quality content also attracts relevant (i.e. qualified) traffic to your site. The more content there is for people to enjoy and engage with, the longer they will stay, and the more they will discover on your website — through repeating this process, your customers are more likely to have a good impression of your brand, your website, and your products. When it comes to the final sales process, it will be a lot easier because they are already familiar with you as a brand and trust that you will provide even more of the high-quality content that they have been enjoying. Because of the law of reciprocity, they are more likely to reciprocate your action of giving them free, high-quality content and will consider buying from you.

Content marketing is also about boosting your publicity. You will want to become well known and authoritative in your niche and target community. You can do so by staying active in community forums or writing guest posts on industry blogs. Although the impact is hard to quantify, branding opens up many unexpected opportunities, such as joint ventures between you and similar businesses to cross-promote each other's products, and implicitly makes selling easier and more convincing.

In this information age, people are always hungry for more content. However, to stand out among the many blog posts, tweets, pictures, videos and other forms of media available on the Internet, creating high-quality content is of utmost importance, and I hope I have emphasized this point enough to ingrain that in you. Of course, this does not happen overnight and is not a one-off strategy. It's about building content over a long-term period on various platforms, including your website and social media, to gradually improve your online presence, increase traffic, build audience and engage with the community. It is about establishing yourself as a brand and finding your place in the crowded online world. But trust me, because content is so integral to the information business, your results will be sustainable and your efforts will pay off.

## Blogging

*Potential result:* Free, targeted traffic

*Input required:* Continuous investment in building and optimizing content

*Pre-requisite:* Topics and niches of interest for target audience

One of the best ways to build content is by blogging. Blogs have been around on the Internet for a long time, and the number of bloggers is steadily increasing. There are plenty of people who write blogs purely out of interest or use them as personal diaries and updates. But from an Internet marketing perspective, blogging is a highly powerful platform for audience engagement, content delivery and sales. So how exactly do you make money from a blog? There are several ways to do so, but a lot of it comes down to building an audience and knowing what content to put on your blog keep them engaged. The formula is to consistently deliver high-value content that helps your audience. If you offer enough content on your blog, occasionally you can drop a sales pitch of your product.

Say, your product is a video course that helps people to master their sleeping patterns and get the highest quality of sleep. What you can do is to maintain a blog on sleep — for example, mention how important it is to have a good night's sleep, talk about the bad habits that damage sleep, discuss what brain activities go on while you are asleep and so on. If you build enough anticipation, excitement and buzz around the area, then the moment you launch a product you don't have to do a lot of active selling, because the selling has already been done in your blog series. When people are reading the content on your blog, they are taking in that information and processing it. You are giving them time to digest what you have posted, and you are not being pushy.

Do you see what this is doing? In essence, you are educating your audience about the importance of good sleep and the damages caused by poor sleep. Then, you come with a solution and a product that will solve the problem. This is how you can make your blog profitable. The concept is similar to e-mail marketing, but with blogs you can put in more rich-media content, pictures and videos, and have a platform where people can leave comments and interact with each other.

A blog is a natural way of capturing an audience. When people look up certain information or search for solutions on the Internet, they might discover your blog and realize that what you have posted is not only answering their particular questions but perhaps also expanding their knowledge. So they might want to subscribe to your newsletters and start following your blog, which helps to expand your e-mail list. Some bloggers also create buzz by doing lucky draws, giveaways and other creative marketing campaigns. Do research into the best blogs and the blogs that you follow, and get some inspiration from them.

Furthermore, a blog has extremely great SEO benefits, because you are constantly creating relevant content. The more related content you create, the more likely will Google's search algorithms 'see' your blog as a relevant topic on a particular keyword. Again, in your blog posts, incorporate keywords strategically and be mindful of the keywords and search cues that you want to target. If your posts are generating enough buzz, and you get lots of people talking about them, reposting and sharing them, it would then create links back to your blog and contribute to your off-page SEO.

Two types of blogs work well. First is the expert blog, where an expert presents an authoritative opinion over a certain topic, and people would learn from that person and imitate his or her successful behavior. This kind of blogs usually have great content, but they can sometimes seem very distant for a lot of readers because these bloggers position themselves as experts of a certain niche. Most people reading their blogs are trying to learn from them, but are not quite there yet.

Another type of blog is the learning-to-be. Nowadays, the Internet presents a low barrier of entry, and people who are not experts can also start their own blogs. If you are working your way up, learning to become an expert on a certain topic, you can document your progress and each step of your learning. Say, your goal is to become a celebrity chef in Japanese cooking. You may not be a celebrity chef right now, but you are learning and trying your best. You can post pictures of your failed attempts, talk about those hilarious kitchen disaster moments and document how each attempt is getting better. This record of your trial and error is almost like creating a documentary or reality show. This gives a sense of authenticity and makes you more approachable to your audience. When you one day succeed in becoming a celebrity chef, or making a beautiful and tasty dish, people will be able to relate a lot more easily. Your example can be a great inspiration for others to do the same. So, be authentic, find your voice, and have a lot of fun.

Once you become one of the top bloggers in your niche, not only can you sell more of your products and services, but corporations and potential joint venture partners will also approach you with business ideas. A blog is visible, searchable and open to anyone who uses the Internet. It is not like an e-mail list where only people on the list will get the exclusive information. Many corporations are happy to send free samples to the top bloggers, because having their products reviewed on popular blogs is an effective and cheap marketing strategy. As these bloggers have already built a relationship with their audience and positioned themselves as a trustworthy authority, their messages are a lot more powerful.

Alternatively, you may start receiving joint venture partnership requests from people who wish to tap into your vast audience base. It can be very lucrative if you structure the deals properly, where perhaps you get a percentage commission of their product sales from your audience or you can request them to return the same favor on their audience list. Thus, having a well-known and highly viewed blog is a way to get free samples, and potentially free sponsorships and deals that you have never imagined were possible.

### Video marketing

*Potential result:* Ability to harvest high-quality traffic, as online videos are becoming a dominant media format

*Input required:* Effort in creating video content on topics relevant to your niches

*Pre-requisite:* Video-recording device

YouTube is the world's number two search engine just behind Google, with 6 billion hours of videos being watched on YouTube every month. Many people see YouTube as an entertainment platform where they watch cat videos or upload the video games they have recorded, but video marketing has become one of the most important trends in online marketing. Using YouTube and other platforms to do video marketing in the right way can massively benefit your business. It is a powerful way increase awareness of your brand and boost your sales. Once you have uploaded a video, it will keep redirecting traffic to your website, bringing a constant stream of income without you having to do more work.

Best of all, video marketing on YouTube can give you SEO benefits. Because Google owns YouTube, every time you upload a video, it gets an unfair advantage whereby it can occupy a higher position in search results. Google has a biased interest to drive large volumes of traffic to YouTube, so that advertisements on YouTube become more attractive to advertisers and more profitable to Google. Moreover, compared with other websites, a YouTube video will automatically show up with a thumbnail image and has slightly more real estate on the search results page, making it more attractive to your prospective customers.

So, what kind of videos can you produce? The first are videos in which you talk directly to the audience, present your products and do a sales pitch. However, not everyone is good at appearing natural in front of a camera, and this idea might seem daunting to many. One way to get around this problem is to have someone interview you. This will make your videos look more natural and friendly, because you are showing human interaction rather than a monologue. To make the whole experience of producing a video less intimidating, you can draft a list of questions beforehand, prepare how you will respond and rehearse the interview before you film it. Finally, you can also produce videos in which you don't even make an appearance before the camera. You can create animations or compile various footages and do a voiceover. In fact, you can be very creative here as long as the video is tailored to your business and shows your brand in a positive light. If you upload content to your YouTube channel regularly, you can attract more subscribers — people who are interested in what you have to offer and, most importantly, your prospective customers.

As YouTube videos are a powerful way to boost your SEO results, it is crucial to optimize the keywords of your videos. The name and descriptions of your YouTube channel, the title of your video, the description and the comments below the video all contribute towards SEO and should therefore be as relevant and keyword-rich as possible. It is important to ensure that your content is clear and consistent, and to engage with your subscribers by replying to their comments, so that every aspect of the customer experience is enjoyable.

## Social media marketing

> **Potential result:** Positive impact on marketing and sales processes
>
> **Input required:** Continuous branding effort through multiple avenues
>
> **Pre-requisite:** Web and social media presence

Social media, when used appropriately, can be a powerful tool to brand yourself and your company, as well as to engage your leads and existing customers. Many people use social media as a virtual outlet to tell the world about their daily lives or rant about their days. While there is nothing wrong with expressing yourself on social media, if you are completely honest, how inspired and fulfilled do you feel after browsing through selfies and cat videos on your Facebook News Feed? Probably not very much.

Given how important social media is in our modern-day society, it is very important to be strategic about what you post, both on your personal account and on your business account. How you present yourself and how you interact with your followers all say something about you as a person and about your business as a brand. It is all about building and maintaining your reputation, and having a consistent online presence.

Social media is where a lot of people gain their first impression of you and your brand. When most people browse their Facebook News Feed or Twitter feed, they skim through a lot of content and will only look at the ones they find interesting, which means you have only a very short amount of time to influence how people perceive you and to get your message across. This is why you should always think about the message you are trying to portray through your posts and try to make it as clear as possible. Pictures are especially powerful, because visual images are perceived more quickly than words, and this is why Instagram and Pinterest are good platforms to use if your products are visual (say, a food or fashion blog).

If you see a picture of someone having a meal with a celebrity, you are most likely to think that that person is also famous. This is what we call branding by association. Who you hang out with, the places you visit and so on will all affect how people perceive you. Only associate yourself with things that are congruent with your brand, so that you are building and reinforcing a consistent image. Similar to what I said about brand inconsistency earlier, if your social media persona is incongruent with your brand, your followers will easily feel confused and distant, and you will find it much harder to build loyalty.

If you don't have a specific niche yet, start thinking about what image you want to present to the world. What is your role and your stance? What do you want everyone else to regard you as? Do you want people to think of you as a great friend or an expert? Post things that will reinforce your brand and avoid showing yourself in a light that does not help with people's impression of you. Most people are attracted to nice, happy and positive things rather than whiny and pessimistic thoughts, so use your social media platform to inspire others by sharing powerful quotes, positive stories and pleasant experiences.

If you have a specific niche that you are targeting, then it is important to brand yourself as an authority and an active member of that community. Post things that are relevant and engage with the community. Spend time replying to people's comments, like other people's posts and comment on them. The more you are involved, the more attention you will get, and more people will become aware of you and your brand, even though they might not necessarily become your customers. Social media is primarily a channel for branding, so the goal is not so much about converting customers but more about building up your reputation.

Because everything can be posted instantly on social media, it has immense power to build and destroy. I am sure we have all heard stories of people being fired after ranting about their bosses on social media, or someone's reputation being ruined overnight after they had posted something stupid or offensive. In the digital age, as soon as you post something on the Internet, it will be read by someone, somewhere in the world, almost instantly. The world is always watching and reading what you post. Therefore, if you want to succeed, you need to be extremely careful about your reputation and manage your online presence well. Think twice before you post something and consider whether what you are about to do will reinforce your image and your brand. If you need an outlet to rant about a bad day, confide in a friend instead of firing your angry thoughts on social media. A good reputation can take years to build up, but only one bad Facebook post or one offensive comment to tear down. And because things can be shared and reposted so easily on social media platforms, there is virtually no way to remove the bad traces. Always use social media to build, not destroy.

The key to successfully acquiring free traffic is creativity, and what I have covered here is just a broad overview and is by no means exhaustive because of space constraints. Figure out where people are spending time on the Internet and try to get ahead of those traffic sources in innovative ways. Of course, consumer behavior will change over time, so you also have to stay on top of the trend and ride on those waves while they are still going. Another important factor is to obey the rules of the large media platforms and traffic sources, so that you do not get punished algorithmically and can keep harvesting free traffic from them. Once you have driven enough free traffic, generated plenty of sales and built up your list, paid advertising is the next step to exponentially grow your business.

**GET PAID TO PLAY™**

## 5 - THROWING YOUR HOUSEWARMING PARTY IN STYLE

### Scaling up with paid advertising

Paid advertising is one of the most important and guaranteed ways to drive traffic on the Internet, provided that you are willing to invest some money up front. The traffic volume is directly proportional to the amount of money you are willing to invest. The key is, of course, to do it profitably and not overinvest on paid advertising to the point where your marketing campaigns are bleeding money and are unprofitable.

To measure the effectiveness of your paid advertising campaign, you first need to define what a "conversion" is on your website — in other words, the key objective of your website. For instance, if your website is simply a lead generation tool for your business, then a conversion for that campaign could simply be a registration or an e-mail opt-in. But if your website is an e-commerce site, where you are selling a product or service, then a conversion is typically a transaction. Defining a clear objective for your paid advertising campaign is crucial, whether this is to drive more leads, increase brand awareness or boost sales, as this allows you to appropriately measure and optimize towards a website's key performance indicators such as conversion rate and return on investment.

## Paid Advertising models

Once your website is functional and has the ability to convert visitors into leads or customers, the next step is to decide which paid advertising platform to use. There are significant differences in the ad's format and in the demographics of users across different platforms. Depending on your goal, different advertising models might be more suitable. I will briefly go through some of the widely used ones here, but this chapter is by no means an exhaustive list of all paid advertising platforms and products.

Pay-per-click advertising is currently the most dominant model. Google, Bing and Facebook are the largest media platforms (also called ad publishers), and Google AdWords, Bing Ads and Facebook Ads Manager all mainly operate on this model, where you define the maximum amount you are willing to pay per visitor (also known as a "click") from the ad publishers' site to your site. This maximum cost per click is also known as the "bid". Your bid, in combination with other factors such as Quality Score in AdWords, determine how competitive your ads are, relative to your competitors', for the best ad slots on the publishers' site. Pay-per-click advertising is a highly effective way to acquire visitors to your site. But because you have to pay for every click, it is more suitable for direct response marketing in order to measure and justify the cost of ad spend and its return on investment.

By contrast, if you simply want to improve the reach of your message or to brand your company, pay-per-thousand-impressions (also known as pay-per-mille) is perhaps more suitable. In this context, an impression means a view of your ad, and you are willing to paying a certain amount of money to get your ad viewed 1,000 times. Your ads can be in the form of display advertising with banner ads that appear next to related content on various websites, or in the form of sponsored tweets on Twitter Ads that can generate more Twitter followings and retweets. This model is most effective on platforms where the commercial intent is not clear. For example, when people go on YouTube, Facebook or Twitter, they are usually just browsing around and don't necessarily intend to make any purchases. By contrast, when people search for specific queries on Google, they usually have the intention to look for certain solutions to their questions. Therefore, your goal with pay-per-thousand-impressions is to inspire, to create brand recognition and awareness, and to blast your message out to a wide audience, as opposed to directly capturing visitors to your website.

Different media platforms operate on slightly different models, but most of them allow advertisers to bid for online advertising spots. For example, Google AdWords is the tool that lets you advertise on Google platforms, usually in the form of ads that are displayed at the top and on the side of search results pages, on YouTube, on Google Maps and on other search network partners of Google. Whether you get the prime real estate on Google's search results pages depends on how much you bid and on the quality of your ad (which I'll discuss in detail in the next section). You could also advertise on Facebook, where your ads mainly appear in the form of sponsored post in the News Feed or as a display ad on the side bar. This is especially powerful on mobile devices, as the News Feed gets more attention on the smaller screens than they would on a desktop browser. Because you can access a lot of demographic information on Facebook based on the groups people join and the posts and pages they like, it is easier to create customized content to make your ads more targeted and effective.

Irrespective of the marketing model and advertising platform, it is important to set daily budget caps to levels that you are comfortable with and are willing to spend. Set a maximum cost per click and maximum cost per thousand impressions so that they are within profitable range on a per-unit basis. This means that for every click or every thousand impressions, you are achieving the desired profit margins. Regularly analyze different metrics (such as impression, clicks, conversion, click-through rate, conversion rate, cost per click, cost per thousand impressions, revenue per click, revenue per thousand impressions, revenue, cost, profit margin and profit), monitor how well your marketing campaigns are running and adjust accordingly to your profitability targets. Make sure you are attracting the right customers and getting a good return on investment.

Paid traffic can sometimes be expensive, especially if the niche you are targeting is extremely competitive. The car industry and the insurance industry have some of the most expensive clicks, costing up to US$50 per click in some countries. Because the market is becoming more saturated, you could potentially be competing with many large corporations who are spending thousands or even millions of dollars on one particular keyword. As someone who is just starting out, it is almost impossible to be ranked near positions one and two, but this doesn't mean you will fail. Even if you may not be able to afford such a high position, you can still benefit from 'breadcrumb traffic' at slightly lower volumes. With paid advertising, you just have to be more careful about your advertising spend and ensure that the financial and operational results are worth the marketing investment.

## Google's suite of advertising products

*Potential result:* Large volume of targeted traffic with strong commercial intent

*Input required:* Continuous optimization through data analysis and interpretation while campaigns run on autopilot

*Pre-requisite:* Small advertising budget and knowledge of paid advertising models

Google's suite of advertising products are some of the most powerful traffic sources for both new ventures and large corporations. Google is by far the world's largest digital advertising provider, taking 55% of global advertising dollars in search alone. Specifically, Google's search advertising business is roughly 6 times that of the next largest search engines, including Bing and Baidu in China. Its market shares for other digital advertising formats are equally strong. You can of course explore other search engines to gain incremental growth once you have exhausted some of these Google advertising products, particularly the more regional players like Bing, Baidu, Yandex and Naver.

Many of Google's advertising products are managed centrally via Google AdWords, including paid search, display network, native Gmail ads and YouTube. Local business owners can even consider using AdWords Express, which is a simplified version of AdWords that is easier to set up than AdWords. Google Grants even offers non-profit organizations up to $10,000 per month of advertising spend for free! This portfolio of advertising products together provide a plethora of ad formats, including text, image, rich media and video.

With Google's search ads, you target customers' search queries by creating ads and bidding on keywords (i.e. combination of words) that are relevant to your business. For example, if you own a musical instrument store, you can target search queries related to buying guitars using keywords like "cheap acoustic guitar" and "electric guitar prices", and place a bid to compete with other advertisers who have bid for the same keywords for the prime real estate — positions on search results pages and other ad networks that are more likely to generate traffic to your website. In this case, customers who search for "cheap acoustic guitar" on Google.com will probably see multiple advertisers' text ads appear at the top and right-hand side of the search results page. Remember to review all of your campaign settings — such as geographical, language and device targeting — and make sure they reflect your advertisings goals and relevance. In fact, having specific, niche-targeting combinations ease the cost of competing against sophisticated advertisers and the complexity of your campaigns, reporting and data analysis. Set very conservative budgets when you are first starting out too.

When building keywords, pay particular attention to which match type you are using. There are four main match types that serve slightly different purposes: (1) Exact match keywords only target the exact search queries and their close variations, such as misspellings and pluralities. (2) Phrase match keywords target search queries that contain the keywords as a string (i.e. search queries with additional words before or after a keyword's string will still be captured). (3) Broad match keywords target search queries that are remotely related to the keyword (for example, the keyword "maps" might capture queries related to travelling and driving). (4) Broad match modifier keywords only capture queries that contain all of the words inside a keyword but does not need to be in any particular order.

The key here is to only create keywords that describe closely what your products and business are, and then find the most relevant landing page from your website to land your leads on. You can do so by reviewing your own inventory and website, research your competitors' keywords and use AdWords's Keyword Planner tool. It is also important to make sure you have control over exactly which search queries will lead to your ads being shown while maximizing traffic source coverage, so that you only capture highly-qualified clicks and do not waste money on irrelevant clicks. Think through your keyword strategy, as your keywords are the basic building blocks of your campaign, and use AdWords's various reporting tools to help you optimize and fine-tune your traffic. A high-quality AdWords campaign is always rewarded by strong Quality Scores, therefore helping you to achieve better positions at lower cost per click.

A text ad on Google AdWords is one of the simplest ads on the Internet, and yet it has probably generated the most ad revenue to these large search engines. In fact, Google relies heavily on profits from its advertising business to fund other futuristic projects like the driverless car. This is all because text ads provide advertisers with the ability to directly address searchers' needs and commercial intents expressed through their search queries at exactly the moments they are researching into them, rather than simply displaying banner ads later on the basis of their demographics, interests or past behaviors on the Internet. In essence, advertisers can create several ads for a specific product. The limits are 25 characters (including spaces and punctuation) for the ad's main headline, 35 characters each for sub-headlines like description line 1 and description line 2, and 35 characters for the display URL (note: it does not have to be a working URL but should contain information about where searchers might land if they click on the ad). Ad extensions, including review extensions, ad sitelinks and call extensions, are extra information that enhances the ad format and visibility. They significantly increase the attractiveness and click-through rate of the ads, and you should definitely utilize them as you see fit for your business. The rule of thumb for ad-copy writing is to ensure the contents (all components of the basic ad-copy and all relevant ad extensions) are highly targeted to the search queries and reflect your business accurately. They should also provide more credibility to your business, in order to convince searchers to click on your ads. The interesting trend to note is that Google and other search engines are now pioneering keyword-less search advertising products, like Dynamic Search Ads and AdWords Express, to dynamically create ad-copies for advertisers and to automate the set-up and optimization of paid search ads. In fact, this is simply part of a much larger trend called programmatic advertising, where the buying, placement and optimization of digital ads are fully automated, and it replaces the need for human optimization.

Once you have created keywords with specific landing pages as well as relevant ad-copies, you will then need to place bids (most advertisers use the default maximum cost-per-click model). Depending on your own financial forecast, unit economics and marketing budgets, you should then work out how much you are able and willing to pay per click. Some keywords and search queries are inherently more likely to reward you handsomely. The keywords themselves and their performance metric offer you hints on searchers' commercial intent and willingness to pay. Do some data analysis yourself or speak to me if you are not sure which bids to place. Alternatively, you can use AdWords's internal automated bidding solutions or external pay-per-click bid management software, or simply start with a very low amount like US$0.20 and slowly ramp up until you reach your profitability target. Obviously, the trial and error method is not ideal and definitely not suitable if you are serious about making the Internet work for you, but it might be the most cost-effective way if you are just starting out and not sure how to analyze your numbers yourself. The holy grail of bidding is to align your unit economics exactly with your bid so that each keyword and search queries are achieving your profitability target, before scaling up your campaigns. You can, otherwise, waste a lot of ad dollars very quickly.

A key feature of AdWords that makes Google's search ads so powerful is that it is not always about who has the most money or who is willing to bid the most for certain key words, it is about the quality as well. Google has devised its own Quality Score to assess the click-through rate, your ad quality, the relevance of your keywords and landing page relevance, and a few other metrics. The rank of your ad among the search results and its position on the page is determined by a formula that multiplies your bid by your Quality Score (from one to ten). By having a high-quality ad, you are essentially getting a discount and can pay less to get the prime ad spaces. Therefore, optimizing your ad quality, bids, keywords and landing page experience will improve your Quality Score, so that you can maximize your return on investment and punch above your weight when competing with companies who can afford large marketing budgets.

The Google Display Network places display ads on a variety of news sites, blogs and other niche sites across the Internet to generate more traffic and potential customers. Online display ads are is similar to ads at a bus stop, on a billboard, on shop fronts and so on in the offline world. In online marketing terms, display marketing is all about online real estate. You can use Google's Display Ad Builder tool to create text, image, rich media (with interactive elements) and video banner ads, or design these ads with the help of outsourced workforce and professional designers (see Chapter 7 on outsourcing).

By selecting appropriate categories, topics of interest and further segmentation, such as demographics, on Google Display Network, your ads will appear in the most relevant places on the Internet and attract people who are most likely to respond. If you are reading an article on a home improvement blog and come across ads selling DIY tools, make no mistake: the advertiser have specifically targeted that blog. Similar to ads in the offline world, display marketing is a great way to build brand and product awareness. Although your display ads might not appear at the moment when your target customers have the intention to purchase, you can still market your products and convey your message to create a lasting impression of your brand. If your brand is memorable and well known enough, then people are more likely to remember you when they have the intention to buy similar products and choose you over your competitors. Don't forget that the Internet is an ecosystem. If you know where to advertise in this ecosystem and how to get different marketing channels to reinforce each other effectively, you can enlarge your net to capture more potential leads and increase your brand awareness.

YouTube is an interesting advertising platform because it has features of both search ads and display ads. YouTube ads can be targeted to specific customer groups on the basis of their demographics, location and interests. Similar to Google's search ads, TrueView ;in-display ads appear on YouTube search results, on the video watch page or on YouTube's homepage. If a user clicks on the ad, they will be redirected to the video page or to the channel. Like display ads, TrueView in-stream ads usually appear before or during YouTube videos or other videos, games and apps in Google Display Network.

As viewers can choose to skip the video ad after 5 seconds, you will only need to pay if they watch 30 seconds or more of the video ad or when they engage with the ad (for example, by clicking on the link to your product). These ads are commonly regarded as "the most annoying 5 seconds on the Internet" — unsurprisingly, the first 5 seconds are the most important part of your video ad. As opposed to traditional TV advertising, with commercials almost equating to toilet breaks, it is much easier to capture viewer's full attention. The vast majority of viewers will finish watching the first 5 seconds, or even the whole ad, in anticipation to the video they want to watch next.

Video is a universally accepted media format and its reach does not exclude those who are unable to read (for example, small children or people with poor eyesight). If your ads are creative and engaging, they can generate a large following and buzz on social media, and can drive video shares and generate subscriptions to your video channel. All of these are hugely beneficial to your brand and can build trust and rapport.

## Paid traffic on social media

**Potential result:** *Targeted traffic based on demographics and interests*

**Input required:** *Creative ideas for viral campaigns; continuous optimization through data analysis and interpretation while campaigns run on autopilot*

**Pre-requisite:** *Small adverting budget and an understanding of the differences in audience and behavior on each social network*

People often wonder why Internet marketers advertise on a whole range of channels and platforms, both paid and free. The short answer is that they all bring in a new stream of traffic from the seemingly infinite and rapidly growing number of Internet users. The more sophisticated answer is that, depending on which channel they came through, customer behavior, intents, and demographics are fairly different; hence, the ability to leverage different marketing channels and traffic sources directly broadens your customer base and reaches potential leads where they 'hang out' on the Internet.

At this point, you may ask, "What is the point of paying for traffic on social media when you can update posts and tweet for free?" It is because algorithms on the likes of Facebook and Twitter attempt to curate the most relevant content for you on the basis of your interests, demographics and past behavior. Therefore, sometimes your posts do not reach every single one of your Facebook friends or Twitter followers. This is a real obstacle if you wish to build viral social media campaigns on demand (unless you are Justin Bieber, have silly cats at home, or have many ice buckets to spare). Reaching your target audience and artificially creating 'word-of-mouth' are made easier, however, when you can pay for advertising and distinguish your posts from the 'sea of sameness' on social media.

Paid advertising on social media also makes sense because it allows you to reach an audience that isn't easy to find on, say, Google paid search advertising. You might inspire and convince these new leads to purchase from you when you accelerate your branding efforts via paid traffic. For instance, there are many Facebook Groups dedicated to antiques, but those enthusiasts and experts are most likely to search for specific queries like "antique southern French silver spoons from the 18th century", as opposed to generic queries like "antiques" or "French antiques". It is nearly impossible to effectively advertise these specific queries on Google paid search, or you may end up with millions of 'long tail', useless keywords that you can only hope and beg for one impression. But imagine if you target those antique enthusiasts based on similar pages they have liked and display your antique portfolio with beautiful images, you just might inspire enough to click onto your website.

Many social media platforms now offer their version of paid advertising, and this non-exhaustive list should give you a flavor of what's available. Contrary to Google, they offer a wider variety of ad formats and pricing models. Twitter offers the chance to promote your Tweets, accounts or trends, and may charge per click, follow, engagement, app install, acquired lead or video view. Facebook Ads offers the ability to target certain interests, devices, locations and demographics, via custom audience (people you already know and do business with) or lookalike audience (users who are similar to your existing customers and people who like your Facebook page). Finally, LinkedIn's Sponsored Updates gives you an extended reach to a professional audience group, different from most other social media platforms, and allows you to target precise job titles, functions, industry, size, seniority and so on.

Always bear in mind how the audience differs from platform to platform on paid and free marketing channels, and tailor your ads and campaigns accordingly. You should also adopt the scientific method to hypothesize, experiment, measure and roll out when it comes to paid advertising on the range of social media platforms. In fact, as more customer data are collected via our devices and various online accounts, audience is such a powerful layer of data for

Internet marketers to segment, target and potentially re-market to.

## Re-marketing

> *Potential result:* Laser-targeted traffic with high potential return on investment
>
> *Input required:* Technical set-up of customer-tracking codes
>
> *Pre-requisite:* Data on customer behavior and customer segmentation

Have you had an experience before where you have browsed a website on a certain topic, and then a few minutes or a few days later, you see ads that are directly related to what you have browsed before? It may seem like a freaky experience, but this is what we call re-marketing, which is essentially done through "cookies". A cookie is a piece of code sent from a website and stored in your browser; it is a marker that identifies you as someone who have visited the website and particular sections of it. When you then go to other affiliated websites, those websites can also pick up the cookie and customize information for you on the basis of the websites and sections you have visited before. This is how websites can show you ads that are directly relevant to what you have searched for in the past. For example, if you have been searching for flights to Rome, then you are likely to see relevant ads of flights, holiday packages and hotels in Rome because you fit into a certain category of customer that the advertisers are targeting.

Re-marketing is becoming more advanced in the online world, and it is a great way to recoup some of your initial lost traffic. It is slightly more technical than other marketing methods and involves deployment of cookies and tag management systems, which will allow you to tag and categorize your customers with some simple codes and to target them with customized content. Cookies are an extremely powerful instrument of your marketing toolbox. If you think about everyone who visit your website, perhaps only 5 out of 100 people will convert and buy your products. Although this 5% conversion rate is an amazing statistic in the Internet world, what about the other 95% of people who left the website without purchasing anything? Maybe it is just the timing that wasn't right. Maybe they did not have a credit card ready at that moment. Maybe your offer page wasn't convincing to them at that particular time. With re-marketing, the aim is to target these same visitors again in the hope that they will come back to your website and become your customers. The return on investment on re-marketed customers tends to be much higher than newly acquired customers too.

Of course, cookies can also help you to re-market to the 5% of people who have purchased from you before. Although they are already on your e-mail lists, what if they don't read the e-mails you sent? With these customers, apart from targeting them with your e-mail updates, you can also re-target them through customized ads, with the use of cookies, when they visit your affiliated websites. These previous customers, and perhaps loyal customers, are perfect to re-target again: if they have bought from you and are satisfied with your products, then they are more likely to trust your brand and buy from you again. Although cookies are slightly more technical for new Internet start-ups, I would recommend doing so as soon as you have the capability, because re-marketing is a powerful way to re-capture relevant customers who are more likely to make a purchase from you.

### Paid advertising on mobile devices

*Potential result:* Optimized marketing methods for mobile devices, as they are surpassing desktops and laptops to become the pre-dominant device type

*Input required:* Effort in building marketing campaigns in formats that are suitable for mobile device screens and in continuously testing new campaigns

*Pre-requisite:* Understanding of how mobile devices differs from desktops and laptops in terms of customer behavior and user experience

As I mentioned earlier, usage of mobile devices such as smartphones and tablets are rapidly surpassing desktops and laptops, and will only continue to become the more dominant device type in the future. Many of the principles I have discussed in previous sections also apply to mobile web marketing when it comes to traffic generation and driving people to your mobile website. However, because many ad publishers (such as Google, YouTube, Facebook and Twitter) display their ads differently on mobile websites, you will need to adjust your advertising strategies accordingly.

First, the ad formats often look and feel significantly different on mobile devices versus desktop browsers. For instance, a landscape banner ad might work well on desktops but might be too wide for mobile devices; hence, ad banners in portrait format are more versatile and optimal for both device types. Another example is to avoid using small fonts on your advertising banner ads, because those fonts may look even smaller and illegible when appearing on a smartphone screen.

Second, ad positioning is different on mobile devices. For example, on desktops, Google AdWords's paid ads fill up the top and right-hand side of the search results page. However, on mobile browsers, these ads only take up the top three spots: the fourth slot is featured at the bottom of the page, requiring users to scroll several times with their thumbs before seeing that slot. These nuances should be taken into consideration when determining your budget size and how aggressive your bidding activities on Google AdWords are. Using a data-driven approach, you can optimize your geographical, language and device targeting, ad formats and bidding accordingly to deliver the desired return on investment on each platform, device type and traffic segment.

Nowhere is the concept of a lean start-up more applicable than in online marketing. As opposed to offline advertising, where small businesses often struggle to compete with the large corporations for the prime ad slots and locations, the online world is a more level playing field. The Internet has enabled businesses with all kinds of marketing budgets to benefit from the huge amount of online traffic. Even if you cannot afford paid advertising at the beginning of your start-up journey, there are still many effective ways through which you can acquire free traffic. As you grow your business, you can gradually ramp up your marketing investment and efforts depending on your budget and needs. Again, once you find the techniques and models that work, don't reinvent the wheel after that. Simply cut the inefficient use of resources (both time and money), and rinse and repeat the actions that lead to transformational results.

## 6 - Networking With Your Neighbors

### Boosting your income with affiliate marketing

As I mentioned in Chapter 2, building your own online sales funnel is one of the most profitable ways to make money consistently. It is because you can then up-sell, down-sell and cross-sell additional products to your customer base, as well as tailor your customers' experience by communicating directly to them through certain e-mail sequences and sales loops. However, product and content creation can be very time-consuming. It takes a lot of work to create all the different products at various price points, and then to move up the ranks to sell the higher-ticket items. Moreover, building a smooth and sophisticated sales funnel will take a lot of effort, such as building follow-up e-mail sequences for each customer segment and persuasive sales pages suitable for your target audience. For beginners, there is actually a much easier way for now.

The usage and penetration rate of the Internet is going up globally. According to Statista, there are 3.17 billion Internet users worldwide in 2015, and this figure will only keep growing. It is not possible to identify every single user from the pool of 3.17 billion users who are interested in certain products and services. Since it is almost impossible to keep up with this growth and capture all the traffic, a lot of companies and Internet marketers are willing to pay high commissions to people who can drive more traffic to their websites. Therefore, one of the best ways to make money online without building your own sales funnel is by being the one who drive such traffic, and this is what we call affiliate marketing.

## Leveraging other people's sales funnel

*Potential result:* Commission earnings from promoting other companies' products and leveraging their sales funnels

*Input required:* Ability to drive quality traffic to the relevant sales funnels and products

*Pre-requisite:* Traffic sources and/or audience in similar niches, such as lists of e-mail addresses

Affiliate marketing is a business model in which you get paid a commission if you can successfully promote another vendor's products and services by driving converting customers to their sales and offer pages. All businesses want more traffic. In the offline world, businesses open shops in the busiest districts and do promotional activities to attract more footfall into their shops, whereas online businesses are desperate for more traffic and clicks into their websites. To capture every single potential lead would be extremely expensive through your own marketing efforts. From my own digital marketing experiences at Expedia, Inc., Google's top 5 advertiser in online marketing budget, even the largest corporations cannot do it all themselves. There is always 'breadcrumb' traffic for other advertisers. This is why affiliate marketing is a viable yet simple business model with limitless potential in the Internet ecosystem.

In the online world, vendors are usually very generous, and commission for affiliate partners often ranges from 30% to 100%. This is especially common for digital products, because there is essentially no additional variable cost, such as manufacturing and shipping, to produce and deliver them over the Internet. If the vendors also have deep sales funnels with higher-ticket items in the back end to sell later or operate on a recurring payment basis, they are often willing to offer 100% commission for the first billings of the entry-level-price, front-end items, as they can make profits for themselves later. Generous commissions are the best way to keep affiliate partners motivated.

The best type of affiliate programs are the ones that let you also monetize on subsequent, back-end purchases from the original leads that you drove to them. Say, you drove 100 leads into the sales funnel.

Of the 100 leads, 50 of them bought the initial $5 e-book and you got 100% commission (i.e. $250). Let's say 20 of them went on to by a $50 product a few weeks later, and you still get a 50% commission (i.e. $25) of each purchase even though you only contributed towards the initial traffic — this will give you $500. As these customers progress down the sales funnel, they pay higher and higher prices, and you still get a commission from those purchases. Of course, the commission might not be as much as 50%, but even a 10% commission of a $5,000 product will give you $500. All of these commissions add up to a generous income, and remember, it all came from the initial customers that you drove into their sales funnel. This is a classic example of how, in the digital age, doing the work once can give you rewards over and over again, without you having to any more work.

Another type of affiliate program to look out for are the ones that give recurring payments — for example, when the product is a membership site or a subscription plan. After the initial commission of 60–70%, you can still get paid 10–20% of commission on a monthly basis, and such a recurring payment is a true source of passive income because you are not doing any work for that money.

Building multiple streams of revenue can make your income more recession- and crisis-proof, and affiliate marketing is often the best way to maximize your streams of revenue from the same action. It is a fantastic add-on to your main source of Internet-generated income, because the nature of affiliate marketing makes it difficult to do in complete isolation. It usually takes little effort to drive additional traffic to your affiliate partners.

For example, if you already have a website that sells gym equipment, you can easily post a link on your website or social media channel to your affiliate partner's online health food store. If you think about it, the people who are interested in buying gym equipment are also likely to want to eat more healthily. Essentially, with affiliate marketing, you are tapping into your existing customer base to sell your affiliate partner's products. You simply need to redirect your customers to your affiliate partner's website, and let their sales system and sales funnel do all the hard work for you. When you drop a qualified lead into their website, a code will identify you as the source of the lead; when that customer converts, you get paid. It is as simple as that.

Affiliate marketing is really a win–win situation: both the vendor and the affiliate partner benefit from such a business relationship. Remember, it is one of the easiest ways to make money without having to build the sales funnel or do most of the hard work yourself.

## Earning commissions through your own site

*Potential result:* Commission earnings from promoting other companies' products and leveraging their sales funnels

*Input required:* Ability to drive quality traffic to the relevant sales funnels and products

*Pre-requisite:* Traffic sources and/or audience in similar niches from your own online presence, such as social media followings and audience from blogs

To earn affiliate commission, you have to find creative ways to drive traffic to your partners' sales funnel and product sales page. And the traffic usually comes from either your website, your own customer base (say, your e-mail list or social media followers), and other promotional efforts to place the affiliate links strategically all over the Internet.

If you don't have your own e-mail list or website now, you can start driving traffic by starting with your YouTube channel, Facebook page or other social media platform, and refer your followers to your affiliate partners. The problem, however, is that your audience is still held in third-party properties, and there is a risk that you will lose them if these third-party sites change their policies or are shut down one day. Additionally, your audience's commercial intent are likely to be much lower when they are using social media than when they are actively browsing products on your website or reading your e-mails.

Affiliate marketing is the easiest when you are already selling your own products or when you already have an e-mail list or social media audience, particularly if the affiliate products are likely to be of interest to your audience. Say, you have an e-mail list of 500 existing customers who paid $100 each for your program on time management, generating a revenue of $50,000. Imagine if you then tell your customers who just purchased your program that your business partner (i.e. the affiliate vendor) is selling a seminar called "How to boost your productivity", priced at $2,000, the odds of them purchasing this product from your affiliate vendor is quite high, because they showed commercial intent in productivity-related products and are therefore considered 'hot leads'. Even if only 30 of your 500 customers purchased that productivity seminar, your 50% affiliate commission alone will be worth $30,000, which is equivalent to 300 additional customers of your original time management program. If you work with affiliate vendors who have deep sales funnels and high-ticket products, then it can be even more profitable for you over time.

If you have an engaged subscriber base to your newsletters, blogs and social media updates, and they trust you as an authority in the field, then they will naturally want to read and find out more about what you have to say. I have emphasized earlier the importance of branding; indeed, when your audience follows your lead and ends up purchasing the vendor's product, the affiliate commission is a direct proof that your branding and positioning are giving you tangible results. This also goes to show how the Internet is an ecosystem, and the different marketing channels work synergistically rather than separately. If you can build a sufficiently large customer base that initially came from your product sales or from your social media following, and if you can inspire and engage them by consistently delivering high-value content, then affiliate marketing is no different from a friendly referral. It does not have to be a pushy sales pitch. Always be on the lookout for great partnership opportunities and invest in building great relationships with your customers so that they trust you as an authority, and affiliate marketing will be a piece of cake.

## Selecting affiliate vendors and products

There are three main ways to find vendors that sell great products and pay generous commissions to affiliate marketers. Most importantly, make sure you partner with vendors and products that are worth your time and effort.

The first is simply to conduct a Google search for "affiliate products", "affiliate sites" or related terms, and to find credible companies that sell high-quality products. This is crucial because you are putting your reputation and your audience's trust for you on the line when you are cross-promoting the vendor's products. Make sure that the products are not scams, are ethical and can deliver the promised results. You will also need to ensure the companies are credible enough that they will not cheat you out of your deserved commission payout.

The second method is to find out from companies that you are currently a customer of, such as Amazon, and join their affiliate program. Most online-savvy businesses have an affiliate program, and the program details are usually located in the small print of their website, near the bottom of the website or in the sitemap. You can search for keywords (press "Ctrl" + "F") on their webpage, or search for the company-specific affiliate program on Google. Usually, the more well-known the company is, the lower the percentage of commission they are willing to pay out, because they usually have larger marketing budgets to spend on other channels and larger traffic volumes. However, don't be put off by the low commission rate they offer. Their strong brand name usually means that your audience will have more trust for their products, and you might end up driving a lot more volume at a better conversion rate when partnering with these well-known affiliate vendors.

The final and most comprehensive method of finding affiliate vendors is via large networks such as ClickBank and CJ Affiliate by Conversant (formerly Commission Junction). The ClickBank marketplace is the world's largest affiliate network, aggregating many of the world's best products, predominantly digital products, with affiliate commission. It is essentially a marketplace where customers can shop for a wide range of products, where product creators can list their products to sell, and where Internet marketers can promote those products and earn affiliate commission. As a budding Internet entrepreneur, you should definitely use ClickBank as a source to find affiliate vendors and a marketplace to list your own products for sale and for other Internet marketers to help you promote. Because ClickBank allows you to have a dual role — as an affiliate partner of other vendor's products and as a vendor yourself — you can generate two sources of income from one website.

So, how exactly should you choose which products to promote? It is worth noting that products on ClickBank are all approved by its internal approval process and legal compliance review, giving you some peace of mind that the products are of a certain quality standard. Once you have signed up for a ClickBank account, you can go to one of the product categories and sort the results by popularity. First, look for high-ticket items. If you sell products at the $5–10 range, you will have to drive a lot more traffic and convert a lot more customers in order to generate a sizeable income. Remember the 80/20 rule? The aim is to find the most effective way of doing something that takes minimal input to give you maximal output. Think about your financial goals, and consider how many items you will need to sell of one product to hit your targets.

Second, look at the average commission per sale. If the commission amount is higher than the price tag of the initial product, this indicates that there is a sales funnel behind that product and that more higher-ticket products will follow. Vendors who have sales funnels are usually more established, and you are also likely to get more commission later when the customers you referred journey deeper into the sales funnel.

Third, look at the average rebill total. This is basically a recurring element — weekly, monthly, quarterly or annual payments — indicating that the product is a potential membership site or subscription plan. By selling products with ongoing payment plans, you are almost guaranteed a stable amount of passive income.

Fourth, always look for products with high gravity, which indicates how successful other affiliates were in selling a product in the last 12 weeks. The exact calculation is mysterious and potentially takes into consideration factors such as the recency of the latest transaction and an affiliate's score. It is also a proxy indication of a product's conversion rate, sales page quality and refund rate. As a general rule of thumb, the higher the gravity, the more success you are likely to have with a particular product.

Finally, look for products that are specific and relevant to your target niche, products that your audience is more likely to be interested in buying. For example, if your product is a healthy diet plan, your subscribers and followers are unlikely to respond if you sell them sports cars. Instead, you will want to promote organic food, cookbooks and kitchen gadgets. Muscle-building products and exercise equipment might also be of interest to your audience. By promoting relevant products, you are maximizing the chance of getting successful sales and creating brand congruence at the same time.

## Establishing joint ventures

**Potential result:** *Win–win situations as a result of synergies from collaboration, usually in the form of financial, economic and relational rewards*

**Input required:** *Research into and collaboration with other complementary businesses*

**Pre-requisite:** *Valuable offering to the other parties, such as a relevant e-mail list of high-value customers*

Apart from using ClickBank and other retail websites to secure affiliate partnerships and products, another way to leverage other people's sales funnel is by establishing joint venture partnerships. These are strategic relationships with other businesses that are selling similar or complementary products and services to yours. The key to win–win partnerships is when the relationship has clear synergies for all parties, and the mutual gains are usually financial, economic and relational.

Going back to the example of selling a healthy diet plan, if your website does not sell the nutritious food and drinks that are mentioned in your plan, then it is a good idea to reach out to the vendors who sell these products. You can also expand your selection of joint venture partners to retailers of healthy ready meals, protein powders or organic produce. On the one hand, by offering your partners' products, you are improving the customer experience: not only can your customers learn about healthy diets, they can also buy the ingredients that they need to follow the plan, all on one website. On the other hand, your joint venture partners can also list your products on their websites and e-commerce channels, developing new sources of revenue for you. In this example, the reasons to collaborate with one another are clear, and all parties are rewarded financially and economically.

By finding joint venture partners who have a natural synergy with your business, you will not appear pushy and the sales process will be smooth. You can be very creative as long as the synergy is clear. For example, if your readership is primarily interested in improving their productivity, you can consider offering products related to time management, reading speed, personal development and so on. The possibilities are endless, but the key is to think from your customers' perspective. If they have been subscribing and buying your products from a certain niche, what are some other things they might be interested in? Would they want to learn about related content through a course? Or would physical products be useful? Two simple ways to find out are to look at the most frequently asked questions in your comment section and discussion boards, and to ask your customers for their views. Their responses can clear some of your doubts and may even ignite your inspiration.

Once you have identified potential joint venture partners, the next step is to reach out to them with a proposal and to construct a deal that will be synergistic and beneficial to both parties. Sell your business and give them samples of your products, so they can also learn more about your brand and see for themselves why you would be a good joint venture partner to them. Know their products and customer base well to present a convincing case of why combining the two lists and sealing such a deal will result in gains for both parties. Agree on a compensation model (the norm is at least 50% commission rate or more for the party that drove the traffic and customers). Remember this: the reward does not have to be purely financial. Relational reward can be just as beneficial, if not more powerful in the long term, including introduction to future business partners or visibility to potential customers on their lists. Make your proposal clear and your case airtight. After you seal the deal, the effort involved from both parties is actually very low, but the potential rewards can be massive.

With the digital revolution comes redistribution of power. In the digital age, power is no longer concentrated in the hands of large institutions and corporations, and individuals are empowered to raise their voice and leverage the limitless possibilities offered by the Internet. As it is impossible to monopolize this huge cyber space and capture all the growing traffic globally, there are always opportunities to collaborate, whether as part of an affiliate program or in joint venture partnerships, with large retailers and small vendors alike. The Internet has lowered geographical barriers so much that markets are now too large to have sizeable direct competitors. Instead of competing for market share and fighting over one pie (under a zero-sum game assumption), a collaborative mindset can actually benefit all parties by increasing the 'size of the pie'. Such partnerships are truly game-changing: not only have they redefined how businesses operate, but they have also enabled many individuals to create passive income and the lifestyle of their choice.

## 7 - HIRING HOUSEKEEPERS AND INVESTING IN ROBOTS

### Outsourcing and automating your business

Scaling up your online business is exciting, but it also involves a lot of work, whether it is driving traffic or building a profitable sales funnel. The good news is, you don't have to do it all by yourself.

The Internet has connected many people across the world and opened people's eyes to the vast talents and skills available in the global Internet economy. Small businesses and large corporations no longer need to put huge efforts into recruiting the right talents in local markets and ensuring that these people are willing and have the legal right to work for them. Instead, they can put up specific job postings to find specialists with the skills for particular tasks, anywhere in the world. This ability to efficiently harness the global labor market and value chain is also more cost-effective. Outsourcing work via the Internet to specialists, rather than to generalists, often means that the best experts in the world can be hired to perform specific tasks, ensuring efficiency and higher-quality output. As opposed to traditional offline businesses, there is no need to pay for the cost of office facilities, computers and equipment.

Furthermore, with the advance of digital technology, automation can solve many business and operational headaches. Many tasks can be automated by programming instructions into systems and software, and the scripts will do all the work for you. Automation allows you to scale up your business without depending on the availability of staff and outsourcers. The nature of outsourcing via the Internet and automation means that you are no longer confined to an office space in a certain location and that more of your time will be freed up: you are truly getting paid to play.

## Why you should outsource

In economics, there is a concept called competitive advantage. To put it simply, people, companies or countries are good at certain things, but they also have their weaknesses. Therefore, they should focus on their competitive advantages and exchange goods or services with someone who has a competitive advantage in something they are weak in. It is most likely that someone else in this globalized economy and value chain is able to produce a similar or higher-quality output with less time or more cost-effectiveness. Maximizing results while reducing time and financial investment is essentially the main reason to outsource. Every one of us is good at something; some of them we are not so good at. By focusing on your strengths, you could really excel in what you do. The things that you don't want to do or don't like doing? You can definitely outsource them to free up your time. For a very small investment, you actually get a much bigger return because you get real results. Imagine if you don't have to work on the administrative tasks that took up so much of your time. Imagine getting someone else to handle the work for you and you just get the end product. The main way to do this is by outsourcing at a very small price.

Outsourcing is often a controversial topic in the media, especially when it is done in an exploitative way, where wages are undercut and labor treated abusively. I firmly oppose this kind of outsourcing, and what I am advocating here is a fair marketplace. On websites like fiverr.com or Elance.com, people put a price tag on the services that they are willing to offer; if you like what they propose, then you pay them the fair price, the price that they put forward. There can be some negotiations here and there, but generally if they're happy to work for a certain price, then it is, in my opinion, only a free market.

Currencies like the US dollar, the British sterling pound and a few other major currencies are highly valued by many countries around the world, because of their monetary worth and stability in the foreign exchange market. These major currencies tend to be fairly stable and are universally accepted. Therefore, many outsourcing platforms charge their customers in US dollar.

The harsh reality, however, is that while US$1 in New York cannot even buy you half a cup of coffee, it goes quite a long way in developing countries. In fact, according to economists at the World Bank, approximately 1 billion people still live below the global poverty line and make less than US$1.25 a day in the developing world in 2011 (1 in 7 people in the world), while 2.2 billion people make less than US$2 a day. This is why many freelance workers are more than happy to take on such projects at a pay of anything from US$5 to several thousand dollars, because they are actually getting a much better hourly pay than what they would get otherwise in their local job market. Those pay ranges are indeed sometimes higher than those of skilled professionals like engineers and lawyers in their own countries. They can also work more flexible hours and pick the jobs they love or are skilled at.

Therefore, don't feel like outsourcing is necessarily exploitation. Of course, if you so wish, feel free to reward your outsourcing partner even more for great results or project outcomes by giving them a tip. When you find freelance workers who work well with your business, it is important to show your appreciation for their work and time, so that you can build great business relationships and a network of contacts that you know will produce great results for your business in the future. Surrounding yourself and your business with high-quality people is critical for sustainable growth.

Outsourcing via the Internet is part of the new reality of globalization, where production of goods and services is no longer restricted by geographical boundaries but by the pure concept of competitive advantage. Whoever can produce the best results in the most resource-effective manner should take on those specific tasks. Outsourcing is the best way to leverage other specialists' expertise. By combining your strengths with other people's, you can really excel.

## Working *on* business, not *in* business

A lot of people look at outsourcing and ask, "Well, if I'm going to pay someone to do it, why wouldn't I do it myself?" First, I will bring the argument of a cost–benefit analysis: how much is your time worth to you? A straightforward formula is to work out your total annual income and divide it by the number of hours you work per year. This way, you will know how much income you generate per hour. This calculation provides a simple rule of thumb. If you encounter a task and wonder whether it is worth doing yourself or whether you should outsource it, just quickly do the math: how much income can you generate in the time it takes to do the task yourself? If it is less than what your time is worth, then outsourcing is probably a good investment. Doing such a cost–benefit analysis can help you decide when it is worth trading your own time for that income.

Second, I would like to introduce the concept of working *on* your business, not *in* your business. Let me explain this a bit more. How often do you find yourself 'firefighting', tackling day-to-day tasks, answering an e-mail here and there, attending meetings one after the other and doing a million other trivial tasks? At the end of the day, perhaps you will feel like you have done loads, but in reality most of the tasks you have done are probably quite small and trivial. You probably won't feel like you have worked and strived closer towards your goal. This is a tell-tale sign of working *in* your business, where you are stuck in the day-to-day operations. Instead, I am proposing a smarter way to work by automating your business, outsourcing it enough so that you as the business owner are working *on* your business, on the crucial aspects of strategic planning, marketing and branding, and doing the tasks that can actually grow your business. This is where outsourcing and automation really come into place, especially in the early days of starting a business, when you have a lot to do and are the only person doing it. If paying US$5 per hour could solve a problem for you, why not outsource it to someone? This has been a game changer for my own business and for many other people's businesses.

I know someone who runs a multimillion-pound business and has more than 200 people working for him, but none of them are his full-time employees. He has a great team of people in India who do all sorts of tasks for him, and he runs his business just like a regular company, where he splits them up into departments, with a project manager overlooking each department's operation. He can enjoy doing what he likes and still has project directors or managers reporting to him, updating him on the activities happening in his business. As a result, he has been able to focus his attention on marketing, branding, strategic planning and product development, looking at where he should take his company next, while not having to worry about the day-to-day operations.

## What you can outsource

So, what can you outsource? My advice here is to simply be very creative. Be imaginative and start small: you can quickly scale things up once you are happy with the results. A few decades ago, it was the manual, low-skilled jobs that were outsourced, especially to countries like India. But as technology advanced, more and more work can be automated instead of done by human beings; therefore, what is outsourced now tends to be work in the medium end of the work spectrum that requires a bit more thinking and more skills — for example, call center work or customer support.

One of the most fascinating phenomena about outsourcing is that many highly skilled people are happy to work in the industry. As I explained earlier, the US dollar is a much valued currency in many countries, and a lot of highly educated people, even those with PhD or MBA degrees, are willing to do outsourced work for foreign companies. What we have started to see is that even legal or accounting work, work that is regarded as highly professional and skillful, has started to be outsourced to countries like India.

Sacha Baron Cohen, the famous actor who played the protagonist in the movie Borat, produced some controversial work and got sued a lot as a result. And because of this high volume of legal cases against him, he is one of the first pioneers to outsource legal work to India. His outsourced legal team in India was in fact trained in American, British and various European laws. Cohen has barristers in the US and Europe who act in court for him, but the more mundane legal work, normally done by junior lawyers, is mainly outsourced. This is a great example of how even the 'high-end' work can be outsourced. This global value chain has fundamentally changed the way we do business in the globalized economy, and it is also a real game changer for many businesses.

As a lifestyle entrepreneur, you can massively declutter your workload and your life by going through a process of elimination. You should literally map out your entire calendar and your to-do list, in order to rigorously go through a process of elimination. Cutting out deadweight tasks and time-consuming activities feel great. Trust me, and try it out yourself!

To get your creative and imaginative thoughts going, let me give you a few examples. You can outsource the drafting of invoices, billing of your products, follow-up of some of your clients via calls or e-mails, or even filing of your tax returns. These types of work tend to take up a lot of time and deviate your focus, directing your attention away from the things that really matter to the growth of your business. Make sure you then place those meaningless tasks into your 'stop-doing list'. If you grow your business fast enough, then these costs of outsourcing would be relatively insignificant. For example, if you can spend one hour growing your business by a few percent that month, you can already afford to outsource more work.

You can also outsource work on a more personal level. A friend of mine wanted to buy a toy that his daughter wanted for a long time as her birthday present, but he could not find it in his local toy shops or on his local Amazon website. Therefore, he gave the precise description of the toy to a worker in India and said, "Find this product for me, and I will pay you for the link." He capped the work to a maximum of 2 hours of research, which cost up to $10 for him. With the help of the outsourcer, he managed to track down the product in under 2 hours to somewhere in Venezuela and was able to treat his daughter to her favorite toy. If he had tried to do the research himself, he probably would have taken much more than 2 hours, judging from his earlier failed attempt. All he did was just ask for help. Not only did he successfully purchase his daughter's favorite birthday present, but he also used those 2 saved hours to spend more quality time with her. He was able to double down on his effort to build a better father–daughter relationship, thanks to the outsourcer's excellent research skills.

This is no different to an executive of a company asking his secretary to buy flowers for his wife or presents for his children. Instead of hiring a secretary who has to be in the same city and same office as you, you just need to outsource the administrative work to a 'virtual' assistant. Of course, do not expect your virtual assistant to mail you your daily morning coffee from wherever he or she works, as it will be cold by the time it arrives. But you can certainly ask him or her to arrange, via the phone or the Internet, a coffee delivery to you from your local café if you are too lazy to get your own coffee.

## How to find and recruit outsourcers

*Potential result:* Very high because it frees up your time,
systemizes business operations and
allows you to scale up your business

*Input required:* Ability to hire and train your outsourcers
to replace your role

*Pre-requisite:* Systematic business processes in place

By this point, you might be wondering, how exactly do
you outsource the work? How do you train and recruit
great outsourcers? One of my favorite outsourcing
websites is fiverr.com. It is a marketplace for people to
list the services they are willing to offer at a flat rate of
US$5 per job. I have personally used fiverr.com for
tasks like graphic and website design. Each vendor has a
score rating, work samples and feedback from other
customers. Make sure you select high-quality ones that
offer you a suitable service as well as appropriate add-
on gigs. You should think more holistically before
engaging with vendors, because it is often better if
vendors can complete the entire task for you end-to-end
via their extra offerings. This is particularly important
for design-related work, in which the initial $5 gig often
will not guarantee unlimited revisions on the design.

Another place to recruit outsourcing partners is
freelancing platforms such as Elance.com and
Upwork.com. On these websites, you post a job with
careful and detailed descriptions of exactly how you

want that done, and most of the time you will get a lot of applications. The challenge is to find people who are meticulous and who can be trusted to deliver a great job for you. The first tip is to look at their star ratings, reviews and profiles when they apply for the job. The second tip is a little trick that I use: within the job description somewhere inline, insert a sentence that says, "If you have read this line, please start your job application with the phrase 'the apple is red'", or whichever random phrase you choose to put in there. What this does is that you can quickly weed out people who are not serious about getting a job or have poor attention to detail (which is a big no-no for many of the manual tasks you outsource), people who did not even finish reading the job description or did not read it carefully. And when all the application e-mails come in a day or so, you just need to filter those with the line 'the apple is red', and those would be the people to pick. This is a great way to eliminate most of the applications. At this point, you can look at their profile, ask them for their portfolio work if it is some sort visual or graphic design work, negotiate turnaround times etc., and select the most suitable one for your purposes. You can also create a series of training videos that describe what your tasks are. By showing these videos to your outsourcers, this simple action can save you countless hours when recruiting in the future. It is as easy as that, and you can be very creative with what you can outsource.

## How to automate your business

*Potential result:* Very high because your business will
continue to run without your active
involvement

*Input required:* Programming codes and software,
written either by yourself or by someone
else

*Pre-requisite:* Relevant software that is helpful to your
objective

Whether it is full automation or semi-automation, software and technologies can greatly simplify your business operations and reduce your active involvement. Thanks to brilliant innovators and technological breakthroughs, the variety of tasks that can be automated is limitless; therefore, it is impossible to create an exhaustive list of how your business can benefit from automation, and what I will discuss next is simply a taster of what is possible. If you come across other useful software that simplifies and speeds up certain operations, scales the business or automates, please share your experiences with me. Details of how to connect with me are given near the back of the book.

Many people think that automation is equivalent to writing a complex computer program to get a certain task done. However, automation is simply defined as an operation that runs automatically with minimal or no active human involvement. It can be as simple and effective as using a dish washer to simplify the process of washing up. You do not need to know much coding or hire software developers to set up simple automated processes. In fact, many of the best automation software comes with intuitive user interface for non-technical users to navigate and use.

For example, you can set up auto-responder, sales confirmation and product delivery (such as links to e-books and online courses) e-mails, as well as e-mail sequences in your sales funnel, using AWeber, GetResponse and Infusionsoft. Apart from WordPress and its plug-ins, you can also use software like Strikingly.com and Wix.com to create your website. LeadPages is a software to create mobile-responsive landing pages and pop-up boxes, and WordPress' own plug-in also have some of these functionalities. With paid advertising campaigns, built-in features of the platforms (for example, Facebook Ads Manager and Google AdWords) often allow you to automate processes such as bidding. You can also use bid management platforms like Acquisio, Flimbu, Kenshoo and Marin Software to dynamically manage your marketing campaigns. To schedule regular social media updates, Buffer and Hootsuite are great platforms to manage your many social media accounts. (The order of tools listed here is alphabetical and does not imply any ranking. Each business has its own needs and budget, so it is important to research thoroughly before you make any investment.)

With both outsourcing and automation, there will inevitably be some initial investment. And with so many tasks that could be outsourced and automated, it can be very draining financially if you try to do everything at the same time. Therefore, always do a cost–benefit analysis to decide whether making such an investment is appropriate. For example, e-mailing sales confirmation to customers after each transaction is very time-consuming and inefficient, and putting in a small investment into an e-mail marketing software could save you a lot of time and effort. But if you only have a small-scale paid advertising campaign, then the built-in software of advertising platforms is probably sufficient for now.

There are many cost-effective ways to outsource and automate your business. The price of these automation software varies widely, and so do outsourcers (for example, professional designers versus those on fiverr.com). You can always start with something that requires little investment and slowly ramp it depending on your business needs. If keeping up with these investments is creating a financial burden for you, then it is defeating the purpose. Remember, the whole point of outsourcing and automation is to make your life easier, not to complicate it.

**GET PAID TO PLAY™**

# 8 - Carpe Diem

## Implementing your action plan

"You pile up enough tomorrows, and you'll find you are left with nothing but a lot of empty yesterdays."

— Harold Hill, *The Music Man* (1962)

It is very, very important to put all these ideas I have mentioned throughout the book into action and see for yourself. Don't just take my word for it. Don't take other people's word for it, especially those who say, "No, you can't do it. No, you should get a stable job. No, you should keep the status quo. Why try new things when you have a fairly comfortable life?" Playing safe is part of human nature, and it is understandable why many people do not want to change the status quo. People dream and expect big things to happen. The problem is, if they do not take action, nothing will change, and it is unrealistic to expect things to happen without any hard work.

Lots of people say, "I know I have a book in me", "I know I can do this" and "I know I can do that". Yet, very few actually achieve the results. A lot of them don't even try; they tend to see what happens and hope for the best. Of course, not all of them will fail, but those who take action are much more likely to achieve their desired results, or even more. There are three types of action takers. First, people who try to do something; second, people who do their best; and third, people who do whatever it takes. It is those who do whatever it takes who will reap the most in life. Doing whatever it takes does not mean taking advantage of others or gaming the system; rather, it is about your attitude and the choices you make. To truly stand out and be unique, give more than your 100%. Sure, you may have to make some sacrifices along the way. It is especially difficult at the beginning when you have to balance your online business with your full-time job. But keep your eyes on the end goal and remind yourself of what is it that you are working towards.

Be open minded and be willing to try new things and new experiences, because the only way you can grow is by stretching and pushing yourself outside your comfort zone, outside things that you already know work and things that you are comfortable with doing on a daily basis. Of course, the disclaimer here is: what I'm referring to here is only the legal and ethical actions, and I will leave that judgment up to your common sense. But within your own value and moral system, try new things. Your experiences are what makes you unique. In my own life, most of the new things I have tried have been a pleasant surprise. I have learned so much from those experiences, and they have played a big part in shaping who I am today.

## Visualizing your goals

To start putting all these concepts and ideas into action, visualize it. Imagine you are financially free. Imagine being able to buy and own the things that you cannot currently afford. Imagine spending less time in the office and more time with your family. Imagine spending more quality time with your friends. Imagine travelling to new places and working from whatever location you like. Imagine having more time to pursue your hobbies and doing the things you are passionate about. Imagine being able to help others to achieve what you have achieved when you are further along the road then they are.

I hope your imagination took you to new places. Visualization is a great aid. Always make your visualization concrete, make it realistic in your mind, and engage your different senses. If possible, try to visit the places that you imagine yourself will be one day. If you want to live in a particular part of town, go there often, immerse yourself in the environment, and imagine what it will like to live there. The reason for doing this is twofold. First, visualization is a great way to test and decide whether your goal is something you would actually like to do. If it is, it gives you even more motivation to get there; if not, it will help you to redefine your goals.

Second, psychologically, by visualizing what is possible, you are training your mind to believe that your goal is within reach and that it is much closer than you think it is. Our mind is very powerful, and our thoughts, whether conscious or subconscious, dictate our actions. So, if your mind limits your hopes and beliefs — if it tells you, "Oh, you can't do that. You will never be rich. You can't possibly quit your job. You can't have your own business…" — then your actions will naturally follow. Your mind will also affect your motivation levels by producing rewards. If you have enjoyed an experience, you will remember that as a reward and will naturally want to do more of it.

## Making concrete plans

After you have identified specific goals, have a concrete plan that will help you get there. This planning requires you to be extremely detailed in what you want to achieve and specific in what you need to do. Here, I'd like to emphasize the hierarchy: set goals to define what you aim to achieve in the long term (say, one year), and divide this timeframe up into measureable milestones to monitor your progress. To turn these goals into action, set objectives to define what you need to do each day to be one step closer to your destination, and break down these objectives into tasks, which are essentially the minute steps towards achieving your objectives.

Part of this planning is about knowing your numbers. Do some calculations and know how many units you need to sell per day to achieve your financial goals. Let's say your goal is to start an online business and grow it to $100,000 this year. How many units do you need to sell by the end of the month, and how many units do you need to sell by the end of the year? At what price points are you selling these products? If these numbers don't add up, then perhaps consider changing the price points, increasing the value you provide to customers, driving more traffic, improving conversion rate or creating a new product line, etc. It is really important to get your numbers right, so you won't ever find yourself in a surprise situation where you realize your numbers never added up. If so, your plan would never have worked even if you followed it exactly.

Every now and then in your journey, do a milestone analysis to measure your progress and benchmark whether you are behind or ahead of schedule. Having these measurable milestones will help you think five to ten steps ahead of competition and ahead of your project, so you are always mindful of your progress and can put your current objectives and tasks into perspective. It is also important to plan ahead of time and factor in the realistic time it takes to complete certain tasks, whether it is done by yourself or someone else. Having a concrete timeline and a strategic plan allows you to coordinate projects between yourself and other people, so you do not have to wait idly for others to turnaround their tasks. Many tasks can be done simultaneously — for example, while you are developing your products, you can hire someone to write your website and another person to design your business logo at the same time.

Another part of having a concrete plan is about setting objectives for each day and prioritizing them. Many people have to-do lists, but most of the time the items on the list are jotted down in a random order as the thought pops up in their head, and they just complete one task after the other without really thinking about what the real priorities are. Although to-do lists can be a helpful tool, it is much more important to prioritize your objectives and tasks before you start doing them.

Imagine cutting a circle into four equal quadrants and labelling them as (1) urgent and important, (2) urgent but not important, (3) important but not urgent, and (4) not important and not urgent. The urgent and important things are the things that really matter. A good way to think about this is, "What is the opportunity cost? If I don't do this, what am I losing out on? If I spend my time on action A, am I missing out a lot by not doing action B?" If action B seems more enticing and needs to be done more urgently, perhaps switch gears and do action B instead. Put away action A for now and reassess later. For example, if you are starting your online business, building your website would be an urgent and important goal, because having a functional website is absolutely essential before you can continue to build your business.

Deciding between the second and third quadrant is a bit trickier — how do you draw the line between what is important and what is urgent? Say, you need to do your tax returns or file your documents into the right folders. They might seem important at first glance, but think about your goal. Will doing these things help you achieve your goal of growing your business to $100,000 this year? While it is still necessary to do these tasks that might come with deadlines, they are not considered important in the big picture. These urgent but not important things don't tend to help you achieve your goals. In this case, it is probably best to do them later in the day. Know the hours that you work best — your 'prime time' and most productive hours — and do the most demanding tasks in those times. Most people are most energized and productive in the morning. If this is you, spend your morning on strategic planning and devising new marketing campaigns when your head is clear, and leave the mindless tasks and easy decisions for the late afternoon. Ultimately, you want to focus your energy and the best part of your working day on the things that are truly important, the things that require your expertise, knowledge, creativity and strategic thinking. However, what's even better is that if the task can be outsourced and you have the resources to do so, then you can use these hours to play instead.

Knowing how to declutter your life and your to-do list is, by definition, a critical component of lifestyle entrepreneurship.

As for things in the final quadrant — the not important and not urgent — you probably don't need to do most of it. Consider outsourcing or automating them, or even throwing them out completely. Most e-mails would fall into this quadrant. Instead of going through your e-mails one by one, replying to some, filing some and deleting the rest, you can create rules in your inbox so that e-mails from a certain sender or containing specific keywords will be automatically filtered and moved to subfolders without clogging up your main inbox. Unroll.me is a useful tool that allows you to unsubscribe certain e-mails or automatically curate them into one big daily e-mail. By doing so, you have essentially prioritized all the e-mails you have to read and substantially cut down on the number of e-mails coming through to your main inbox. Moreover, you don't need to reply to every e-mail right away, and having e-mail notifications can distract you from the task you are doing. You can set aside half an hour each day to deal with e-mails; if those e-mails are important and urgent enough to warrant your immediate attention, the sender would probably have called you. Be disciplined and train yourself to only read and reply to the necessary e-mails.

For each day, have one to two objectives that you really, really want to achieve — the things that, if left undone, will leave you sleepless when you go to bed at night. Focus on these objectives for the day, and when you have achieved them at the end of the day, you will feel highly accomplished because you will have done the things that matter most.

## Managing your tasks

Having set your objectives for the day, break them down into smaller tasks so you know exactly what needs to be done. Think about what you could do to maximize your output. Remember the 80/20 principle? The goal is to find the point at which your 20% of action will turn into the 80% of results. A great habit I have picked up from my time working in the tech industry is this simple action of putting post-its on a board. Essentially, think about what you need to do that day to achieve your objectives, and turn these into tasks that you can complete in 1 hour or 15 minutes. In this way, you can 'time box' that task, setting a maximum amount of time that you will spend on it and thus breaking down a large, improbable task into much more manageable chunks. So, if your objective for the day is to build your website, you can aim to spend 15 minutes on buying a domain name and setting up a hosting account, and 1 hour on building the skeleton of your website using WordPress.

Psychologically, you will start to realize that things are much more achievable when they are broken down into these manageable 1-hour or 15-minute chunks. Every task becomes a lot clearer, and every time you tick off a task from the system, you will know exactly what your progress is. Set your objectives and plan your tasks strategically at the beginning of each day. Then, you can just complete one task after another, rather than having to do a task, pause, think about what needs to be done, and repeat the whole process again. Having an organized system also allows you to keep in mind the big picture and put the tasks you are doing into perspective. It is much better than going down one path and then realizing that you have forgotten or missed something, or having to keep referring back to earlier tasks.

Task management essentially comes down to being selective about what you do and maximizing your productivity. The first concept is knowing what to do and what not to do. The latter part — knowing what not to do — is especially important. As we go through life, there will always be more things, more demands from others than you can ever possibly handle. There are more books in the world that you want to read than you can possibly can finish during the course of your lifetime. There are more businesses you can start, more clients you can pursue. There is more of anything and everything, but the most important thing is learning how to say "no". This is the key difference between successful people and the really successful ones, according to Warren Buffett, the third wealthiest person on Earth. I know it may sound very ruthless or selfish, but let me just ask you this: how much is your own time worth to you? How much is your energy worth to you? Will you spend your life constantly living up to someone else's demands, even when it is sometimes against your own will? As I explained in the last chapter, if you get caught up in the day-to-day operations of your business, it is easy to lose sight of the bigger picture. Determine what you can outsource using the cost–benefit analysis described earlier, and outsource as many tasks as you possibly can.

Even if you are an employee, it doesn't mean you cannot be selective about what you do with your time. On multiple occasions, I have explained to my managers and colleagues at work why I could not commit to a certain task. Why? It's because I don't want to become a 'yes man'. Indeed, sometimes you don't want to be known as the person who says "no" all the time, but if you can frame and position it in a way such that it becomes a convincing case, it can actually become a win–win situation for both parties. Let me explain that in an example.

Many times I have been asked to do some very manual tasks, which I knew would take hours but would create negligible volume for some marketing campaigns

I had been running. When I was given that kind of task, I would often explain, "Okay, I see your point here. But I estimate that such a task will take me 12 hours realistically, and it won't make a big impact on the marketing campaigns. As I'd really like to maximize my impact and make sure my time is well spent, so that you also get the highest return on investment from me, here is another project that will add more value and potentially grow the campaigns by up to 30% in a week. Would you be okay with that? Furthermore, would it be possible to automate your original task with a script, or to outsource it?"

The response I usually get is, "I must have underestimated how long the task will take, and your explanation make a lot of sense." Quite often as well, my managers would scrap the original task altogether. In fact, I have been praised multiple times for being transparent, data-driven and logical in my explanation, and for eliminating inefficient aspects of the business. This is another reason why you should say "no" if there is a genuine reason that a certain task is not worth your own time, or anyone's time, to do.

The second concept is to maximize your productivity. I have been trying to improve my productivity for as long as I can remember. Even as a young boy, I wanted to do things faster and better so that I can fit more things into my life to satisfy my curiosity and enrich my experiences. I liked to play sports, I wanted to volunteer in community projects, I wanted to have a fun social life, and I was also determined to do well in school, finish all my homework and prepare ahead for the next day. I guess you can call me a high achiever, but I attribute a lot of my success so far not to talent but to my desire to improve my productivity, to do more things and to get things done. Therefore, knowing how to get things done and how to manage your tasks is important.

David Allen, in his book *Getting Things Done*, introduced a great idea of putting everything you have to do into a system that can be easily accessed. This prevents us from spending our brainpower thinking about what's next during our downtimes. Instead, by having everything recorded in a system, we can free up that brainpower and be more productive. It is important that the system you use is easily accessible — say, on your smartphone — and is something that you trust and can easily refer back to. iCalendar, Google Calendar, Wunderlist, Evernote and Trello are all fantastic software to note down and organize everything in your personal and professional lives, both in calendar format and a dynamic list format. The fact that they can be accessed on all your desktop, smart phone and/or tablet means that the apps are readily available to you.

This brings me to the point of making every day count. Having a few minutes to plan your day before taking action can be immensely valuable. Every day, before you start doing any work, always make room for some quiet time where you can strategically think and plan your day, and determine your objectives and the exact tasks that you need to do to move your business forward. Every day has to be a transformational day.

## Don't overwhelm yourself

Successful people and highly effective people tend to have one thing in common: they are extremely disciplined in choosing what to do and what not to do, and in following the system that they believe will work. They rarely get distracted; even when they do, they can usually correct themselves very quickly and get back on track. And discipline is something that we all have to learn because if we do not discipline ourselves, we can easily get distracted, lose sight of our goals and feel overwhelmed.

Like I said earlier, knowing how to say "no" is vital to create a healthy life balance and to avoid overwhelming yourself. A big proponent of this concept is Warren Buffett, who is a master at saying "no" to things he doesn't deem important. He does not commit to all the charity or social networking events like other rich and famous people do, and turns down many speaking engagement and invitations. He is very focused on his task of finding undervalued stocks and investing in them, and then growing that investment portfolio. He is a man who much prefers to spend time in his quiet office in Omaha, Nebraska, reading financial statements and keeping up with current events and business opportunities. He leaves the origination of his investments, deal finding and the networking to his trusted advisors and staff, so that he could focus on what he is best at — assessing companies and deciding whether to make the investment — and avoid overwhelming himself with the additional commitments.

Ultimately, the whole reason I am writing this book is to encourage you to get paid to play. Getting paid is only half the equation; the play component is equally, if not more, important. As a lifestyle entrepreneur, you need to understand precisely why you are building an Internet business and passive automated income streams: to enable you to create your ideal lifestyle. The Internet business is not a get-rich-quick scheme. It definitely takes plenty of work and effort, but knowing your 'why' will keep you motivated throughout the journey. While you are working hard towards your goals, don't forget to reward yourself and celebrate your milestones and achievements with your loved ones.

The importance and necessity of rewarding yourself regularly have been scientifically proved in behavioral psychology and economics. Aptly put by Ivan Pavlov in his famous Pavlov's dog experiment on classical conditioning, you can create a positive feedback loop that reinforces and encourages certain behavioral patterns. For instance, every time you make 10 transactions, you can celebrate by going to the movies. And then you can start increasing the target to 100 transactions and reward yourself by going to a nice restaurant for dinner. Later on, you can increase the target to 1,000 transactions and celebrate with a weekend trip. The reward should be proportional to the size of the achievement. As an example, going on a fancy cruise experience when you have only made $100 in profit would seem too overboard. In fact, you would have made a net loss from this expensive reward and would probably struggle to find newer, better stimuli and rewards for future milestones.

Research from the prestigious Wharton School of Business at the University of Pennsylvania offers another rewarding yet productive technique called "temptation bundling". There are two types of behaviors and outcomes: short-term indulgences will usually lead to negative outcomes in the long run (for example, people who commit fraud for quick monetary gain will risk long-term reputation damage), and 'good behavior' that comes with short-term cost will usually result in sustaining benefits (for example, people who are willing to pay the immediate cost of practicing a musical instrument will reap long-term rewards later). The aim of temptation bundling is to associate the short-term indulgences with the long-term benefits. For example, only allow yourself you scroll through your

Facebook News Feed after you have optimized your Facebook Ad campaigns, or treat yourself to watching funny videos on YouTube after you posted a work-related video for your video marketing campaign. The pressure of these Internet marketing efforts will be overshadowed by the rewards afterwards, and you are much more likely to do the right, but often 'painful', tasks. Temptation bundling is a practical way to fight procrastination and accomplish tasks that are important but not urgent. By leveraging your guilty pleasures as incentives, doing the more difficult tasks that pay off in the long run becomes much easier.

### Don't throw all eggs into one basket

While having a laser focus on your goals is important, you also need to scan the horizon for new opportunities and be open minded. If there is one thing that the digital economy has taught me (and hopefully you have taken away from this book), it would definitely be to never stop learning in this rapidly evolving digital revolution. Although these new trends might seem crazy or incompatible with your current business at first glance, you won't lose out by learning more about these trends. You will never know what opportunities are awaiting you until you look and try.

When you decide to take these opportunities, it is important to remember not to 'throw all eggs into one basket'. You would become very distracted if, every time a new trend comes up, you dump away all the hard work you have put into your plan A and jump onto plan B. Also, doing so causes your mind to lose that laser focus on the end goal that you were trying to achieve through plan A. Throwing all eggs into one basket is a very expensive exercise, and you might risk throwing away most of your savings, time and hard work, only to realize later that you have made a wrong decision.

It doesn't hurt to try out a new idea while you are working hard on building your business or having a full-time job. Spend time after work and on the weekends to try it out at a small scale. Commit only a small amount of time and money in the beginning, and you can always ramp it up when you are confident that it is a good investment. This is exactly what the new economy and the digital age have allowed you to do. Take the example of paid online advertising. No matter how big or small your budget may be, you can set a strict daily spend in your marketing campaign so that it does not exceed the amount of money that you are prepared to pay. This is very different from offline marketing, where you must commit several thousand dollars upfront just to get an ad up in the local newspaper for a few weeks. In the online marketing world, you can always start a campaign with as little as $10–50 per day to get some traction. If the return on investment seems decent, then you can ramp it up to

$100, $500, $1,000 and so on. You can grow your marketing campaign without overspending and can know exactly how much you have to pay per day. If the performance is not as expected, you also have the option to modify or pause your campaign with great flexibility.

In the digital age and the new economy, you can try out different things on the side while keeping your main source of income alive. It does not hurt try out plan B alongside plan A, until it becomes successful enough that it can be pivoted into your plan A. However, the word of warning is: never try too many things at once and never lose track of your plan A. Make sure you keep doing the things you are good at and do them well because, ultimately, you still need to secure your monthly income and sustain your current lifestyle. This is a great way to ensure that, even if your plan B fails, you fail elegantly because you always have plan A, something that works consistently.

Although psychologically it helps for you to know that you are 100% committed to something, it is not the smartest way to assess your risks and opportunity cost economically. Your risk appetite will change at different stages of your life and will depend on how much money and resource you have. It is very important to be rational in your decision making. Always assess the opportunity cost and consider whether you are prepared to take the risks. This is why, even though time and financial freedom is the ultimate goal, I do not recommend quitting your job just yet, before you can generate a stable source of income from the Internet.

# 9 - 01100001 01100011 01110100

## Embracing the digital revolution

Throughout our careers and lives, many opportunities will come our way, but more often we will have to find and create opportunities for ourselves. The digital revolution has truly changed the way things work in modern-day society and has brought with it many opportunities. The Internet has empowered and enabled people to generate income in innovative ways, and the barrier of entry has been lowered so much that you don't need much more than a laptop and an Internet connection to benefit from what it has to offer. In this book, I hope I have successfully given you a glimpse into the endless possibilities of how you can leverage the Internet to generate income. More importantly, I hope I have inspired and encouraged you to take these opportunities and create the ideal lifestyle for yourself.

Much of the online world has similarities with the offline world. You can sell physical products on your website, or be a third-party seller of other people's products (drop-shipping). However, the Internet has also propelled us into the information age, and there is huge demand for information products such as e-books, webinars, online courses and membership sites. Underpinning a series of related information products at different price points is an automated sales funnel, which differentiates the top Internet entrepreneurs from the average.

The Internet has enabled individuals to start their online businesses with very little initial capital. Once you have created your website, you can drive free traffic by optimizing your website for search engines, creating relevant content and branding your business on social media platforms. Or if you have a bit more to spend, you can scale up your business easily by running paid advertising campaigns on various search engines, display advertising networks and social media platforms. Moreover, the Internet has also allowed you to grow your wealth by financial trading.

The scale and reach of the Internet has changed how businesses operate. Many online businesses benefit from working together, such as by establishing affiliate partnerships, launching joint ventures or offering your online real estate to other advertisers (Google AdSense). Because there is virtually no geographical barrier, work can be outsourced to anyone in the world. Many aspects of your business operations can also be automated to free up your time and allow you to engage in work that is more creative, innovative and productive.

You can do a lot more with the Internet other than watching cat videos on YouTube, looking at your friends' selfies on Instagram or reading the news. Indeed, the Internet has been one of the most liberating technology ever invented, granting the average person much more power and choice. Because this powerful invention has such flexibility and versatility, there will only be more innovations and better technologies in the future, and it is a serious mistake to not ride on this wave and take advantage of the endless possibilities that the Internet offers.

One of the biggest empowerment of the digital revolution is the ability to design your lifestyle. Many well-paid jobs and professions have demanding hours, and people who have worked hard to climb to the top often had to sacrifice a lot of their time in exchange for their sizeable paychecks. Some companies, especially those in the tech industry, now allow more flexibility for employees to structure working arrangements around their personal or family commitments. However, there is still an unspoken expectation that you have to be in the office during certain hours, so that you can attend most of the meetings and interact with your colleagues. Ultimately, the freedom of choice is still restricted.

This is why the ability to do business over the Internet is such a game-changer. Imagine having the financial and time freedom to do the things that you genuinely love. Imagine going for a morning run in the park without having to worry about getting the early train so you won't miss that 9 am meeting. Imagine doing only the things that you truly love. I am a firm believer of financial and time freedom, because I believe life is too short to not pursue your dreams. Why live a miserable life, or a life doing things that other people expect you to do, when you can enjoy and take control of your own life and your freedom, and really design a lifestyle that suits you, your family and your financial situation?

The title of this chapter is actually the digital binary code for the word "act". You can only succeed if you take action. The beginning of the journey is always the most difficult part but, no matter how hard it is, never give up. Some people might call this stubbornness, but I like to think of it as having a laser focus on the task at hand. Many of the greatest people in history have tried millions of times until they succeeded. This is exactly the kind of mindset I want you to have. If you want to succeed, persevere and do not give up. How you approach the small things is a reflection of how you will do the big things in life.

Always remember what you are striving for. Do not lose sight of your vision, and think about what it is that you are pursuing. Money is only a tool to help you achieve your goals and definitely not the ultimate aim in life. As P. T. Barnum said, "Money is a terrible master but an excellent servant." After reading this book, you should now have a much better understanding of how the Internet fundamentally changes the way we work and live, and how it empowers each and every one of us. I sincerely hope you can take back the driver seat of your finances and time by leveraging the Internet, so that you can truly get paid to play.

**GET PAID TO PLAY™**

# DISCLAIMER

*"No matter how great the talents or efforts, some things just take time. You can't produce a baby in one month by getting nine women pregnant."*

— *Warren Buffet*

I don't believe in 'get-rich-quick' schemes — only in putting in the hard work to grow your business and getting rewarded, adding value and serving others. My book is intended to help you understand how the different online business models work, and how you can leverage the Internet to generate income and to create your desired lifestyle.

As stipulated by law, I cannot and do not make any guarantees about your ability to get results or earn any money with my ideas, information, tools or strategies. Your results in life are up to you. I just want to help by giving great content, direction and strategies that move you forward. While nothing in my book or on my websites is a promise or guarantee of results or future earnings, I am happy to offer my help should you need it — please get in touch to find out more (details at the back of the book).

**GET PAID TO PLAY™**

# GLOSSARY

**80/20 principle:** Vilfredo Pareto's principle that 80% of the results come from 20% of input

**Affiliate marketing:** a type of performance-based marketing in which a business rewards one or more affiliates for each customer brought by the affiliate's marketing efforts

**Bounce rate:** the percentage of visitors who leave the website after browsing only one page

**Click-through rate:** the percentage of people who click on the link to your website out of all who see your website on the search results page

**Conversion rate:** the percentage of visitors who take a desired action; for example, the percentage of visitors to a website who make a purchase

**Domain:** a name, owned by a person or an organization, that is used as an Internet address to identify the location of a particular webpage

**Drop-shipping:** an online business model in which you act as a third-party seller of other supplier's products, which are sent directly from the supplier to the customers' shipping address

**E-mail list:** a list of people who subscribe to e-mail newsletters on a particular topic, which allows widespread distribution of information for branding, communicating and selling purposes

**Google AdSense:** Google's advertising placement service that allows website publishers to display Google advertisements (for example, targeted text, videos or images) on their webpages and earn money when site visitors view or click the ads

**Google AdWords:** Google's online advertising program that allows advertisers to display ads on Google and its Display Network

**Hosting:** An online service that stores all the pages of a website and makes them available to users connected to the Internet

**Mobile-optimized web:** web designs that automatically re-format for use on mobile devices, such as by having larger navigation buttons and optimized positioning of content and images

**Opt-in page:** also known as squeeze pages; pop-up box or landing page on a website that convinces visitors to sign up to an e-mail list

**Pay per click:** a paid advertising model to direct traffic to a website, in which the advertiser pays a certain amount to a publisher for every ad clicked from the publisher's site to the advertiser's site

**Pay per thousand impressions:** also known as pay per mille; a paid advertising model in which the advertiser pays a certain amount of money per 1,000 impressions (i.e. times that the ads are shown) on a publisher's display network

**Sales funnel:** a sales process starting with a large number of customers making an inexpensive, low-ticket purchase and progressively journeying towards fewer customers making more expensive, higher-ticket purchases

**Scarcity:** a sales technique that creates time-limited offers or limits the quantity of products to increase sales

**Search engine optimization (SEO):** an unpaid technique to increase the amount of visitors to a website by obtaining a high ranking in a search engine's results page

**Stop loss:** in financial trading, a stop loss is a specific price point at which you exit the market when the price drops below or goes above your pre-specified range

**Web analytics:** the study of web data to understand how elements of a website affect user behavior. Such data are useful for measuring web traffic, doing business and market research, and optimizing website performance

**Webinar:** short for "web-based seminar", it is a seminar conducted over the Internet using video conferencing software

# ACKNOWLEDGMENTS

First of all, a massive thank you to you, my reader. Thank YOU for supporting this book, and I sincerely hope you enjoyed it and can go forth and make your own waves. This book was written for you and with you in mind: it is the culmination of the expertise of all my teachers and my experience in Internet income generation. I would love to hear from you, both feedback and/or questions, so that I can continue to stretch myself and improve.

To my Mom and my biggest supporter in life, thank you for always being there and guiding me through tough times. Even though you may have worried about me at times, thank you for letting me run wild with my ideas.

To my Dad and my other biggest supporter in life, thank you for giving me encouragement when I needed it the most. My past experiences would not have been as eye-opening without your wise advice and provision.

To Esther at NextScroll.com, you have worked magic and done wonders to my original manuscript during the publishing process. Your professional editing and formatting, as well as tireless work ethics and support, propelled my book and me to new heights.

To Godwin at StructurePractice.com and my artistic friend, Rachel, thank you for your finishing touches and expertise in book cover and graphic design. I need not worry about people judging my book by its cover.

To Raymond, deep gratitude for penning the foreword and for your mentoring and guidance. You pushed me beyond my boundaries.

To Vishal and Naval, special thanks for your kind words and for teaching me so much and being genuinely helpful throughout the publishing process.

To Erik, Michal, Magnus, Roger, Alex and Songnian, a massive shout-out and thank you for your endorsements and quick turnaround time, despite very busy schedules.

I also thank my family and extended family for being my biggest fans.

My sincere gratitude goes to my mentors and managers throughout my career for giving me the opportunity to embark on this exciting journey and for passing on their knowledge to me.

Special thanks to those with whom I had stimulating conversations about the digital economy, and a salute to the pioneers and trailblazers of digital technology and Internet marketing.

Without the inspiration, guidance and support of many people, I would not be the person I am today, and this book would not have been a reality. Whether explicitly mentioned above or not, I am eternally grateful for everything these countless number of people have done for me and taught me.

## FOR MORE INFORMATION AND FREE BONUSES

Digital technology is evolving at an unprecedented speed. While much of the fine details of this book, especially in relation to Internet technologies and products, will probably look completely different a few years from now, the fundamental principles will still stand. The book's website (**www.GetPaidToPlayBook.com**) is regularly updated and is a living continuation of the many strategies and techniques mentioned in this book. As my most valued readers, I have given you many FREE bonuses on the website. GetPaidToPlayBook.com is the authoritative resource that will help to propel you into the 'dot com' lifestyle!

*Facebook: Get Paid To Play*

*Twitter: #GetPaidToPlayBook*

*YouTube and Google+: Get Paid To Play*™

### How can I be of value to you?

Are you struggling with your Internet business or not sure where to start? Would you like more information or hand-holding to kick-start and grow your Internet business?

To follow my work and expertise beyond what's included in this book, please visit **www.KarsenCheung.com**, where you can download more FREE resources too. You can also e-mail me at **Connect@KarsenCheung.com** to discuss how we can work together to achieve better results.

On both of these websites, I will publish relevant examples, stories, best practices, extensions of these Internet business models and other useful ideas.

Please also stay connected on social media.

*Facebook: www.facebook.com/KarsenCheung*

*Twitter: @KarsenCheung*

*LinkedIn, YouTube and Google+: Karsen Cheung*

## Send me your story, testimonial and/or feedback!

Have you had any experience and/or success stories with implementing the strategies and ideas in the book? Would you like to tell me about how reading this book changed your perspective?

If so, please e-mail them to **Stories@GetPaidToPlayBook.com**. I would love to hear from you and connect with you — I promise to read every single one of them!

If you feel that yours or someone else's story might inspire others, I will even consider it for possible inclusion in future books or materials.

Furthermore, I am also humbly open to any constructive criticisms and feedback that you may have, regarding my work and my book. Please send them to **Feedback@GetPaidToPlayBook.com**, and I will do my best to improve and to serve you better.

## ABOUT THE AUTHOR

Karsen Cheung has managed 8-figure USD annual Internet marketing budgets for Expedia, Inc. | Hotels.com, the world's largest online travel company and the top 5 spending advertiser globally on Google. Optimizing and rapidly growing numerous multimillion-dollar marketing campaigns, while acting as the regional lead on bidding analytics, ad-copy innovation and the project manager on product development and automation, Karsen acquired world-class and hands-on digital marketing experiences.

While exploring the depths of Internet income generation, Karsen also built up a successful track record and wealth of knowledge on topics such as trading financial markets online, outsourcing and automation.

Karsen previously worked with Bain & Company (prestigious strategy consulting firm), Procter & Gamble (P&G, largest consumer goods company), ING-Bank of Beijing, the London 2012 Olympic Games, and the UK Office for National Statistics. He also spent time with some of the fastest-growing Internet start-ups and venture capital funds, while acting as consultants for

NGOs, social enterprises and corporates in Germany, Uganda and China.

Karsen graduated from the London School of Economics and Political Science (LSE), University of London, where he found his passion in strategic marketing and consumer psychology. He went on to publish his dissertation on the social psychology of luxury spending behaviors.

Karsen's experience of living in London, Shanghai, Hong Kong and Taipei has destined him to catch the 'travel bug'. Since then, his 'itchy feet' has already taken him to more than 55 countries, and his life plan is to travel to all 193 of them.

His ideal 'Get Paid to Play' trip is outer space travel. In fact, a NASA microchip with his name is sent and currently en route to Mars. It is one way to temporarily deal with this ambitious travel plan until commercial space travel is possible.

He once creatively hitchhiked from London to Malaysia in 24 hours without using any money, travelling a total of 10,500 kilometers on 7 different modes of transport.

**www.KarsenCheung.com**
**Connect@KarsenCheung.com**.